Everyday Life in Renaissance Times

The EVERYDAY LIFE series is one of the
best known and most respected of all
historical works, giving detailed insight
into the background life of a particular
period. This edition provides an invaluable
and vivid picture of the everyday life in
Europe during the Renaissance.

E. R. Chamberlin investigates life at Court;
life in the city and how the aristocracy,
the merchants and the common people lived
and worked. He also examines the wars, the
Inquisition and the Plague; the world of
learning and the world of religion.

3 cde

Other EVERYDAY LIFE books

and published by Carousel Books

EVERYDAY LIFE IN
RENAISSANCE
TIMES

E. R. CHAMBERLIN

Drawings by Helen Nixon Fairfield

Carousel Editor: Anne Wood

TRANSWORLD PUBLISHERS LTD
A National General Company

EVERYDAY LIFE IN RENAISSANCE TIMES
A CAROUSEL BOOK 0 552 54041 2

Originally published in Great Britain
by B. T. Batsford Ltd.

PRINTING HISTORY
Batsford edition published 1965
Batsford third impression published 1969
Carousel edition published 1973

Carousel Books are published by
Transworld Publishers Ltd., Cavendish House,
57-59 Uxbridge Road, Ealing, London W.5.

Printed by James Paton Ltd., Paisley, Scotland.

Note: The Australian price appearing on the back
cover is the recommended retail price.

Contents

The Illustrations

Note: *The italicised numerals in the text refer to the figure-numbers of the illustrations*

Acknowledgment

The Author and Publishers wish to thank the following for permission to reproduce the illustrations appearing in this book:

The Abingdon Press for fig. 122
Staatliche Museen, Berlin, for fig. 42
The Trustees of the British Museum for figs 29, 54, 62 and 95
The Mansell Collection for figs 37, 40, 61, 93, 94, 107 and 112
Foto Marburg for fig. 43
The Metropolitan Museum of Art, New York (Rogers Fund, 1919), for fig. 53
Alte Pinakothek, Munich for figs 14 and 28
Musées Royaux des Beaux-Arts de Belgique for fig. 44
The National Portrait Gallery, London, for fig. 30
The National Gallery of Art, Washington, for figs 13, 15 and 16
The Wilton House Collection for fig. 52

Select Bibliography

ALLEN, J. W. *History of Political thought in the sixteenth century*, 1951
ALLEN, P. S. *The Age of Erasmus*, 1914

BAINTON, ROLAND *The Reformation of the Sixteenth Century*, 1953
BAX, BELFORT *The Peasants' War in Germany*, 1899
BEYLEY, C. R. *Prince Henry the Navigator*, 1901
BOAS, MARIE *The Scientific Renaissance*, 1962
BÖHN, M. VON *Modes and Manners*, Vols II–III, 1935
BRYCE, JAMES *The Holy Roman Empire*, 1921
BURCKHARDT, JACOB *Civilization of the Renaissance in Italy*, 1914

CAMBRIDGE MEDIEVAL HISTORY, Vol. VIII: *The Close of the Middle Ages*, 1932
CAMBRIDGE MODERN HISTORY, Vol. I: *The Renaissance*, 1902
CARTELLIERI, OTTO *The Court of Burgundy* [tr. M. Letts], 1929
CASTIGLIONE, BALDASSARE *The Book of the Courtier* [tr. Sir T. Hoby 1561], 1900
CELLINI, BENVENUTO *Autobiography* [tr. J. A. Symonds], 1948
COLLINDER, PER *A history of marine navigation* [tr. M. Michael], 1954

DERRY, T. K. and WILLIAMS, T. I. *A short history of technology*, 1960
DURRANT, WILL *The Reformation*, 1957

EHRENBERG, R. *Capital and finance in the age of the Renaissance*, 1928

FROUD, J. A. *Life and Letters of Erasmus*, 1894
Fugger Newsletters [tr. P. de Chany], 1924

GREEN, MRS J. R. *Town life in the Fifteenth Century*, 1900
GREGOROVIUS, F. *History of the City of Rome in the Middle Ages* [tr. A. Hamilton], Vols VII–VIII, 1900

HAMMERTON, J. A. (Ed.) *Universal history of the World*, Vols V–VI
HIORNS, F. R. *Town building in history*, 1956
HUIZINGA, J. *Waning of the Middle Ages*, 1948

JACOB, H. E. *Six thousand years of bread*, 1944

KELLY, F. M. and SCHWABE, RANDOLPH *Historic costume*, 1929

LACROIX, P. *Military and religious life in the Middle Ages*
LEO, H. C. *History of the Inquisition in the Middle Ages*, 1888

MACHIAVELLI, N. *The Prince* [tr. L. Ricci], 1903
MADARIAGA, SALVADOR DE *Christopher Columbus*, 1949
MUMFORD, LEWIS *The city in history*, 1961

NOHL, J. *The Black Death* [tr. C. H. Clarke], 1926

OMAN, C. W. *History of the art of war in the Middle Ages*
OSWALD, J. C. *A history of printing*, 1928

PARRY, J. H. *The age of reconnaissance*, 1963
PEDDIE, R. A. *Printing: a short history of the art*, 1927

READE, J. *Prelude to chemistry*, 1906
RENARD, G. *Gilds in the Middle Ages* [tr. D. Terry], 1919
RENARD, G. and WEULERSSE, G. *Life and work in modern Europe*, 1926
ROGERS, J. E. *Six centuries of work and wages*, 1891

SELFRIDGE, H. G. *The romance of commerce*, 1918
SMITH, PRESERVED *History of modern culture*, 1930
SPRENGER, JACOB and KRAMER H. *Malleus Maleficarum* [tr. M. Summers], 1948

SUMMERS, M. *History of Witchcraft and Demonology*, 1926

TAWNEY, R. H. *Religion and the rise of capitalism*, 1926
THOMPSON, J. W. *Economic and Social history of the Middle Ages*, 1928

YOUNG, G. F. *The Medici*, 1909

ZIMMERN, H. *Hansa towns*, 1889

Introduction

THE labelling of historical periods can be as misleading as it is useful. Certain broad trends extending over centuries can be discerned and defined and, for the sake of convenience, these trends may again be subdivided and the subdivisions named after their outstanding characteristics. But here lies the trap: no period starts and ends at a particular moment in time. The roots of each extend far back into the past and the influence of each moves on long past that point of termination which is used for convenience. The use of the word 'Renaissance' for that period of time centred around the year 1500 is, of all labels, the most misleading, for it can be defined in whatever terms the historian chooses.

Jacob Burckhardt, the Swiss historian who first analysed and described the period as a whole, looked upon it as the trumpet blast which heralded the modern world. His view is still accepted by many. But Burckhardt was writing in the nineteenth century and the 80-odd years which have elapsed between his day and the mid-twentieth century have seen far greater changes than the 400 years which separated him from the world of the Medici. There had been changes, but these were not basic. Communication in the nineteenth century was still the laborious transport of matter on wheels or foot over land or on ship over sea; the monarchies which were establishing themselves in the sixteenth century were, with the exception of the French, still powerful in his day; the fighting man on horseback was still the spearhead of armies. It is no longer possible to view the Renaissance as though it were the basis of our own society; its elements are present, even as elements of classic Rome are present, but the court of Augustus Caesar is no further from us in spirit than the court of Lorenzo de' Medici. So far has the pendulum swung from Burckhardt's position, that there are some who would deny the existence of the Renaissance altogether, classing it as the last flowering of the Middle Ages, pointing out that there had been other, and greater, 'renaissances' before that of the sixteenth century.

There can be no doubt that the men who actually lived at that time were vividly aware that they had stepped into a new world. Erasmus, the great humanist scholar who looked upon all Europe as his country, spoke poignantly for them when he cried, 'Immortal God, would that I were young again in this new age that I see dawning'. A Frenchman, speaking with a certain smugness, catalogued the discoveries of the period as evidence of its excellence. 'The world sailed round, the largest of Earth's continents discovered, the compass invented, the printing press sowing knowledge, gun-powder revolutionising the art of war, ancient manuscripts rescued and the restoration of scholarship, all witness to the triumph of our New Age.' Unlike many historical labels, the word 'renaissance' itself was coined, by an Italian, at the time it was needed. It came into use about the year 1550 and shortly afterwards another Italian defined the preceding period as that of 'the Middle Ages'.

Italy was the fountainhead of the Renaissance, for the whole concept of re-birth was the discovery of the classic world of which she was heiress. But all Europe eventually shared in that discovery. Thus, the allocation of an opening and closing date to this period is virtually impossible. If Italy is being discussed, then the opening date could be placed as early as the thirteenth century, while 1600 would not be too late a date for northern countries. Like a great stream which rises in the south and flows northward, it arrived at different places at different times. The basilica of St Peter's in Rome, whose construction started in 1506, and the cathedral of St Paul's in London, begun in 1675, can both be described as Renaissance buildings. The date of 1453 was long used as the opening point, for it was in that year that Constantinople, the great Christian bastion in the East, fell to the Turks. It was believed that refugee scholars brought into Europe those precious Greek manuscripts whose contents sowed the seed of the new learning. But Greek scholars had been abroad in Europe for at least a century before that date and the fall of Constantinople, far from providing a fresh source of manuscripts, put an end to one which already existed. Nevertheless 1453 is a convenient date to employ if only because Europeans were forced to turn to the West, abandoning that dream of conquest which had given rise to the Crusades, after losing their foothold in the East. And if the fall of Constantinople may be taken as opening point, then the Thirty

Years War of 1618–48 can be the close, the two points showing the path which Europe travelled during the 200 years. The struggle for Constantinople was the focal point of the struggle between Christian and Muslim; the Thirty Years War was the struggle between Christian and Christian.

For by the year 1500 Christendom was dead. The ideal of Europe as a single unit, under a single monarch and a single priest, still lingered among scholars, the last pale shadow of the Roman Empire. There had been an attractive but deceptive harmony in that ideal which saw the Pope, Christ's spiritual vicar, as the twin of the Emperor, Christ's general, together holding sway over all Christian men. The reality now mocked the ideal. The Papacy had destroyed the power of the Empire after a merciless struggle for supremacy and sought to control Europe alone, debasing its spiritual for the sake of its temporal powers. And from the ruins of the Empire sprang new nations, dividing the continent with their artificial boundaries, clamouring for a place in the sun.

Chapter I

THE EXPANDING HORIZON

T HE world was centred around an almost landlocked sea. The
Mediterranean stretches some 2,400 miles from east to west,
its width varying from 100 to 600 miles so that it acted as a
bridge, not a barrier, between Europe and the fantastic lands of
Africa. A map of the known lands before the fifteenth century would
show an area of about 4,000 miles from north to south, Scandinavia
and Arabia approximately marking the extreme limits, while to the
west the islands of Britain clung to the very edge of the world.
Beyond these limits were regions of night and terror and fable.
Eastward, and the picture is more detailed and extensive for the
ancient civilisations which had arisen round the Nile, the Tigris
and the Euphrates formed a staging post, as it were, for a European
traveller. Eastward still, and there is a long, narrow belt of known
country, the track followed by European conquerors from
Alexander of Macedon to the Caesars. In their wake, the merchants
followed for at the other end of this track lay precious products—
the silks of China, the spices of India, the incense of Arabia. It was
a public road, but its entrance was private; the great maritime
powers of Venice and Genoa controlled the approaches to the
Levant, its starting point. Only through their hands could the
wealth of Asia find its way ultimately into Europe for their war-
galleys knew only one rival in the Mediterranean, the war-galleys
of the Muslim. Then, in 1453, Constantinople fell, breaking the
link between East and West. A powerful new people, the Turks,
inimical to all Christians whether they called themselves Venetian
or English, Genoese or German, now dominated the eastern end
of the Mediterranean. Trade caravans could pass through along
the ancient route only at their good will. But Europe was hungry
still for those luxuries which only Asia could provide: frustrated
by the Turk, merchants of Europe sought another route.

The new world was opening because the old was closing; there
was no route to the East save that which ran down the African

coast. The seamen who took this route now became aware of a greater challenge and possibly greater opportunity—the endless, grey wastes of the Atlantic beyond whose horizon anything might lie. But before that challenge could be taken up three things were needed: maps, navigational instruments, and ships. All three were achieved by the end of the fifteenth century.

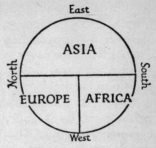

1 The 'T' within the 'O': conventional rendering of *a mappamundi*

MAPS

The view of the physical world current before the Renaissance was based on Biblical sources, closely reflecting the existing habits of thought. It was an enclosed world with neither room nor need for speculation; everything flowed logically from the basic assumption that the Bible contained all that was necessary to understand the physical as well as the spiritual world. Learning emanated from religious centres, and was devoted to religious purposes; it was therefore inevitable that map-makers, drawing upon this main source of knowledge, should produce works with a religious bias. In the medieval *mappamundi*, the Earth was represented as a flat disc with Jerusalem at its centre. Paradise was precisely located in the east, at the top. Europe and Africa lay to north and south, neat triangles separated by water; the Great Ocean surrounded the whole. 'A "T" within an "O" shows the design', an Italian wrote confidently as late as 1422. The 'O' is the world itself, the 'T' is the waters dividing it (*1*). Turned upon its side with the north in the now conventional position at the top, the overall plan is not wildly inaccurate—though greatly simplified. The vertical limb of the 'T' is the Mediterranean, the horizontal limb is composed of the Aegean Sea, the River Don, and the Nile, which together composed the boundary of Asia. The map-makers living in Britain or elsewhere upon the Atlantic seaboard possessed a personal knowledge of the Great Ocean, a sea so huge that the world was scarcely large enough to give it home, and the western coast and islands of Europe therefore appear with some approximation to reality. But, for the rest, details appear as prescribed by fancy, by the Bible, or by garbled news of strange peoples and places brought by

17

travellers. Mount Ararat, sometimes complete with the Ark, always finds a place; so too do Sinai and Jericho, the tower of Babel and the pyramids of Egypt. Beyond the boundaries of the known world were the abodes of fantastic peoples: headless men or men with one single, huge foot under which they sheltered in the noonday heat; men who went on all fours, or had but one great eye, or whose heads were like dogs. Most of these fantasies had some basis in reality, being distortions of local peculiarities of costume or habit. All these were incidental details. The maps showed the great pilgrim centres, gave some slight aid to the pilgrim himself and satisfied the stay-at-home who might want to know the location of Paradise. That was all that was required; there were very few who travelled by land for either pleasure or profit.

It was the featureless sea which men first charted adequately. The limited area of the Mediterranean with its familiar headlands and islands made navigation an easy matter: the shipmaster merely followed the coast. A knowledge of prevailing winds, of currents at the mouths of great rivers, and the ability to identify a few stars at night helped him during the very short periods when he was out of sight of land. But, on the whole, for centuries he travelled at sea from one landmark to another much as his fellow travelled on land. The invention of the compass in the thirteenth century gave him a priceless new instrument which enabled him to travel confidently out of sight of land, and from it developed the portolan, the first true chart. Based on a series of compass roses— points of the compass—the portolan enabled the shipmaster to sail down a compass course chosen in advance. Coastlines were drawn in minute detail and with astonishing accuracy. A portolan chart will show a mass of lettering along the coast and the banks of major rivers, identifying landmarks visible from the ship; inland, no details are shown and the sea area itself is covered with the compass roses which spread like a series of spider's webs. A handbook accompanied the chart, giving sailing directions, descriptions of harbours and the like.

The portolan was ideal for its limited purpose, but without a broader view of the world seamen would have continued to plough up and down the coasts of the Mediterranean and the western Atlantic. There was little point in courting suicide by sailing westward, for the world ended a few hundred miles west of the Pillars of Hercules. But in the second half of the fifteenth century the concept of the world was radically changed. This new concept was a re-discovery, as were so many other scientific advances of the period. Knowledge had been mislaid not lost, and was contained in a few hundred sheets of parchment scattered about the Arab world. It was the work of Ptolemy, a Greek of the second century A.D., living in Alexandria at the time that the Roman Empire was at its height. Merchants and soldiers had gathered an enormous body of information related to their travels over the Empire. Most of this information had been compiled through hard necessity. Military commanders needed to know the swiftest way to get a body of troops from one point to another, how to outguess the tactics of local enemies, how to ensure the safest and most economical transportation of provisions. Merchants following the armies also needed to know the safest and easiest route for their heavily laden pack-animals. Not for another thousand years was the world to witness such a constant coming and going as during the hundred years which preceded Ptolemy. From Britain to India, from the Sahara to the Rhine, men were on the move. At first they

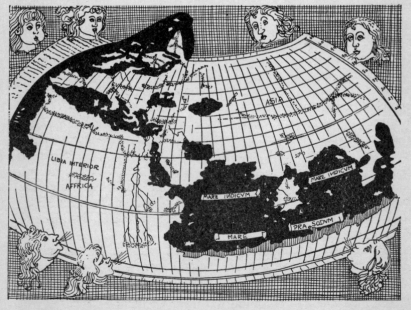

2   Map of the World, reconstructed from Ptolemy's co-ordinates

were dependent upon word-of-mouth information regarding the best routes, but later handlists were compiled for them. Ptolemy was essentially a compiler, drawing together into one comprehensive scheme the notes and observations of scores of anonymous men, summarising it in two great works, the *Astronomy* and the *Geography*. The *Astronomy* entered Europe via the Arabs as early as the twelfth century: the lucrative practice of astrology alone ensured it a ready sale. But the *Geography* remained unknown until it was translated direct from the Greek into Latin, in 1410; thereafter several manuscript copies went into circulation until 1475, when it was first printed.

There were no maps with the manuscript which reached Europe, but Ptolemy had provided co-ordinates for each of the place-names in his lengthy gazetteer, constructing for them the now familiar parallels of latitude and longitude. It was a comparatively simple task for the new race of geographers to follow his instructions and create a more realistic picture of the earth than had been known since the days of Rome(2). The Mediterranean was not only the natural centre of the world but was also a familiar area to Ptolemy, who was therefore able to describe the lands surrounding it with considerable accuracy. Spain seems to be floating away into the Atlantic and Italy appears triangular; but North Africa is distinct and so is the Red Sea, the serrated coastline of Greece and the island of Ceylon. Westward the world ends at the Canary Islands. Neither Ptolemy nor his late medieval followers believed it to be, literally, the end of the earth, so that if a ship sailed westward it must tumble over the edge. Long before, the Greeks had postulated a spherical earth, the centre of a universe enclosed by crystal spheres which carried the stars and the planets. It was only during the long night of darkness over the Western World that the old terrors of a flat, limited earth returned. Ptolemy dispelled that fear—at least for the informed. Columbus knew that the world was round: his illiterate seamen, not unnaturally, wanted proof. They would have been even less happy had they known that their captain's optimistic calculations were based upon a fundamental error. Ptolemy had miscalculated the length of a degree in establishing his parallels of latitude, estimating that it was one-quarter shorter than it was in fact. The new maps based upon his *Geography* naturally followed the error, with the result that Asia was immensely broadened, apparently coming to within 3,000 miles west of Europe.

India and China were the goals of the first navigators. If it had been known that half a world of water and a great continent lay between the shores of Europe and China even Columbus might have been daunted.

NAVIGATION

Throughout the early fifteenth century ships were cautiously probing their way down the western coast of Africa, and eventually rounded the Cape of Good Hope in 1487. But even though ship-masters now measured their distance from their home-ports in thousands instead of hundreds of miles, they were still coastal seamen who ventured out of sight of land with the greatest reluctance, their navigation still based upon the compass and portolan chart. It was not until 1581 that any distinction was made between pilotage and navigation, between the skill required to take a ship through known waters and that required to travel thousands of miles over open sea. A shipmaster was his own pilot and naviga-tor, drawing upon traditional knowledge and his own personal knowledge of local conditions. Almost illiterate, he was yet immensely learned in his trade, carrying the whole encyclopedia of nautical lore in his head, assisted by only two instruments, the compass and the lead.

The curious properties of the lodestone had long been known, but it was only in the thirteenth century in Europe that its magnetic qualities were embodied in a practical device for seamen. Tradi-tionally, the compass was supposed to have been developed in the Italian port of Amalfi and was at first little more than a straw or chip of wood, bearing a magnetised iron needle, which floated in a bowl of water. By the end of the fifteenth century it had become a more precise instrument, the needle mounted on a pivoting card marked with the compass points. The lead was probably a contri-bution made by northern seamen. The clear waters, good visibility and comparative regularity of the Mediterranean seabed made visual sounding simple, but along the Atlantic coast the opaque-ness of the water, accompanied by bad visibility through many months of the year, made some kind of non-visual device essential. The lead was the answer—a chunk of metal varying in weight from 7 to 14 lb., depending upon whether it were to be used in shallow waters inshore or in deep sea. The line to which it was secured was marked off in fathoms by knots, and in the base of the lead itself

3 Swinging the lead

From an ornamental title-page

was a hollow filled with tallow which would pick up samples of the seabed when it touched. Swinging the lead in shallow and possibly turbulent waters required considerable skill(3). The great length of line was coiled and the seaman, standing as far forward in the bows as possible, heaved the lead ahead of the ship, allowing the coil to run out after it. By the time that the ship had caught up with the lead, the leadline was perpendicular and the leadsman could call out the depth of water signified by the last knot remaining above the surface. Hauled in, the tallow at the bottom was examined to see the nature of the material which adhered to it. The lead acted as an eye for the shipmaster in familiar waters, confirming his knowledge of the area over which he was sailing. He would know that at a given spot the depth should be so much, the bottom covered by fine sand, shingle, mud, as the case might be. In unknown waters the lead could save his ship, giving warning of sudden shoals.

Compass and lead were sufficient for passage through familiar or coastal seas. But, as voyages grew ever more adventurous, and familiar landmarks disappeared over the horizon, some form of true navigation began to be required. No seaman had yet taken the challenge and turned the bows of his ship westward but, during the rounding of Africa, it was obvious that much time would be saved if passage were made direct across the great bays instead of following the coast. During such a passage, land would not be visible for perhaps days on end and some means of establishing position was vital. Two elements were required to achieve this: knowledge of the distance sailed from the last known point and the time taken. The first true dead reckoning was not undertaken until late in the sixteenth century, nearly a hundred years after Columbus had crossed the Atlantic. He and his predecessors had learned to estimate speed by the time taken to pass a piece of floating debris or an observed headland. Considering that the principle of the knotted leadline was already well known, a curiously long time elapsed before the basically similar log was evolved. Initially, this was merely a handy piece of wood tossed into the sea, whence estimation of the ship's speed could be made as she passed it. It was common sense to tie a line to the log in order to retrieve it and later knots were tied to the line at regular intervals, and a flange fixed to the log in order to increase its resistance to the water. When the log was 'streamed', the speed at which the knots ran out was timed with an hour-glass. Logging at regular intervals provided the master with a passably accurate estimation of his average speed. Such simple navigation was based on the assumption that the ship was travelling in a direct line. This ideal situation rarely occurred: a ship might be blown off-course or the master might deliberately alter course with a favourable wind. There could be many alterations of course, at the end of which an attempt at dead reckoning would be impossible. A simple but effective record of course alterations was provided by the traverse board, a wooden board with 32 radii, one for each compass point, along which were bored eight holes. At every half-hour of his watch, indicated by an hour-glass, the helmsman would insert a peg in one of the holes of the compass course upon which he was steering. At the end of the four-hour watch each alteration of course would be thus apparent and could be recorded.

In 1490, the world was still limited to the area Ptolemy had known over 1,200 years earlier; by 1521, the globe had been circumnavigated and a ship had sailed upon every ocean. The great voyages of exploration undertaken during these thirty crowded years were made by seamen using the crudest instruments supplemented by traditional lore. The scientific discoveries taking place on land had very little effect on seamanship even though these discoveries were of great and immediate value. Seamen are among the most conservative of people; no better indication of their traditionalism can be given than the survival of such humble terms as 'log' and 'knot' when applied to the navigation of a modern vessel equipped with electronic aids. The seamen of the early Renaissance were further hampered by illiteracy. Most could spell out tables of sailing directions and possessed a personal knowledge of the movement of celestial bodies, but few had the mathematical ability needed to take advantage of the new discoveries in astronomy. Nevertheless, even before the great global voyages were undertaken there was a

4   The quadrant

pressing need for more precise navigation. Voyages were financed not for the love of exploration but for the hope of financial profit; a seaman who discovered, but was unable to return to, some wealthy country would find scant sympathy from his financiers. It was a comparatively simple matter to proceed down the African coast by dead reckoning, but some method was needed to 'fix' a discovered land so that it was possible to make landfall there whenever required. The fixed reference point was found in the most enduring feature of the universe, the stars themselves. These were, for all practical purposes, fixed bodies and therefore, as an observer moved away from one of them, its angle relative to himself would change in a constant ratio. The cold bright glory of the Pole Star made it an obvious choice; shipmasters had already observed that its angle, or altitude, grew steadily less as a ship moved south, decreasing by approximately one degree for every sixteen leagues sailed. The quadrant and the astrolabe, two instruments which had been long in use by astronomers, were adapted to enable seamen to determine the polar altitude at any given point. The quadrant was simply a quarter circle, marked from 0 to 90 degrees on its curved surface, with two sight holes on the straight edge and a plumb line descending from the apex (4). The star was sighted through the peepholes and the angle read off from the point where the plumb line intersected one of the degree marks. It was a difficult instrument to use, for if the ship were rolling heavily the plumb line would swing, making it almost impossible to read.

The astrolabe overcame this difficulty. The astronomer's version of this instrument was a beautiful and complicated device used to plot the movements of the planets. The seaman's astrolabe was little more than a metal ring—indeed, it was frequently termed a 'sea ring'—marked off in degrees and with a movable metal rule across its centre (5). It was not held in the hand but was suspended from a cord and it was an easy task to sight the star and move the ruler accordingly, reading off the angle marked by its intersection with the degree mark. A development of the astrolabe was the cross-staff, consisting of a squared staff some three feet in length, marked off in degrees and with a movable crosspiece furnished with two sighting pegs. The staff was held to the eyes and the crosspiece moved until it precisely fitted the apparent space between the horizon and the celestial body under observation. It was accurate and could be made by any ship's carpenter but of all navigational instruments it was the most trying to use. The long length of staff had to be held, without wavering, while the horizon seemed to rise and fall; if the observer blinked he might lose the precise moment of reading and have to start again. The backstaff, or Davis quadrant, later embodied the principle of these sighting devices in a more manageable form. The observer stood with his back to the sun so that its shadow fell upon a graduated scale.

5　Mariner's astrolabe

The various methods used to establish degrees of latitude worked with tolerable accuracy; all attempts to establish longitude failed totally. Columbus believed that a table of magnetic variations would provide the answer; Amerigo Vespucci spent nearly a year trying to establish a method based on lunar movements. The only possible method is based on exact timekeeping, and it was not until the invention of the chronometer in the eighteenth century that the task was accomplished. All that a Renaissance shipmaster could do was to 'run down the latitude', that is, to cast around until he had found the latitude of his destination and then alter course to east or west and sail down it.

SHIPS

The man who provided the impetus for the first great voyages of modern history was essentially the last of the Crusaders. Prince Henry of Portugal, called the Navigator, was born in 1394 and died in 1460. He was a young man of twenty-one when he was made governor of Ceuta, the stronghold opposite Gibraltar which the Portuguese captured from the Moors in 1415. News came to him there of great wealth to be found in the interior of Africa and along the western coast, of the gold and ivory and slaves which determined men could gain. He was fired, too, with the ambition to outflank the Moors, the great enemy of Christendom, and contact at last the legendary figure of Prester John. This John was a king so great as to disdain the ordinary title of king and styled himself simply 'priest'—Presbyter John. He counted seventy-two monarchs as his subjects; in war he could place more than a million men in the field; in peace there was no dissension throughout his kingdom. Before his great palace hung a marvellous mirror in which he could see all that was happening throughout his vast realms. The legend of his being had haunted the consciousness of Europe ever since the Muslim had begun to hammer at the gates. Some day, it was said, this great Christian prince would arise in the rear of the hordes of Mohammed and sweep them into the sea. His country was variously located, but most men agreed that it was Ethiopia, the strange land of black Christians which was even older than Rome. Neither Henry nor any other man ever found Prester John, but the search for him precipitated a wave of exploration. Henry established a species of college in Sagres in Portugal where all were welcome who could throw light on the problem of how men could find their way around the globe. Seamen and astronomers, merchants, mathematicians and shipbuilders, all had something to contribute, Sagres acting as a clearing house of nautical lore.

But, though it was Portuguese ships which first descended the African coast, rounded Africa and opened a new world, the hunger for new lands was not confined to one nation. The research of the few became the property of the many, and that which the Portuguese learned, swiftly became available to all Europe. In spite of the national jealousies which inspired them, the voyages of discovery were essentially international in application: a Genoese by the name of Columbus, after peddling his dreams to the kings of England and Portugal, at last became a viceroy of Spain. By the time that the Spanish monarchs generously allowed him to commandeer three tiny ships, Africa had been rounded and the deep Atlantic penetrated—for the Canaries were re-discovered in 1415 and the Azores discovered in 1445. It is highly probable that at least one vessel had, involuntarily, crossed the Atlantic and returned, for, throughout his planning, Columbus gave every indication that he knew that land lay between 3,000 and 4,000 miles west of Europe (6). Somewhere to the west lay the East; all

6   Columbus landing in the Bahamas

that was needed was a stout heart and a stout ship. He could provide the first; the second, too, was at hand.

A recurring factor of the Renaissance is the almost miraculous timing of crafts which came to fruition at the precise moment they were needed. The Vikings may have discovered America centuries before, but that discovery had little practical value because it was then impossible to maintain regular communication. Even in the fourteenth century, the most competent and enthusiastic seaman could have done little more than dream about the possibilities of crossing the Atlantic, for the ships available were not equal to the task. The birth of the full-rigged ship between 1400 and 1450 was as revolutionary an event as that which ushered in the age of steam in the nineteenth century. The full-rigger was the child of two distinct traditions; broadly speaking, the Mediterranean produced the hull and the Atlantic provided the rigging(7). The Mediterranean tradition of shipbuilding was at least 3,000 years older than that of the Atlantic coasts of Europe, but throughout the greater part of that time emphasis had been laid upon propelling a vessel by means of oars. The Romans harnessed the tremendous, free power of the wind for their merchant-men, but the galley remained the fighting craft. Its manœuvrability and

7   A full-rigged ship

independence of wind, together with its capacity for high speed over short distances, ensured that it was employed for certain purposes long after the full-rigger was developed. The battle of Lepanto in 1571 was the last true battle between galleys, but this highly specialised warship found a place in most navies until the end of the sixteenth century and even lingered on into the eighteenth century. It was also employed to transport precious cargoes of small bulk—but it was highly expensive, roughly one man being required for every ton of cargo carried. Considerations of economy were immaterial in war but were obviously of prime importance to any would-be explorer. The quantity of foodstuffs needed for perhaps two hundred men over many weeks, made the galley an impractical vessel for Atlantic voyages greater than those attempted by the Viking longships.

The vessels developed in the north lacked the clean, elegant lines of those of the south, for they were intended to withstand the boisterous conditions of the northern seas. Their characteristic shape was squat and sturdy, with a square sail set upon a single mast. In the Mediterranean the lateen sail still held its own; it was a huge triangle of canvas which permitted a ship to sail very close to the wind but required a large number of men to manipulate. The lateen remained for faster vessels, but the seamen of the south adopted the northern square rig for heavier vessels. Some time before 1400 the rudder had been adopted universally in place of the single, huge sweep which was almost unmanageable in heavy seas. The rudder, hinged and with a tiller, required a square stern and it was only then that ships acquired the distinction between bow and stern which is still evident. Gradually, improvements from north and south resulted in one basic vessel, a craft with three or four masts and five or eight sails. The great expanse of canvas provided enormous power, but with it came the problem of ensuring that the canvas met the wind at the angle and to the extent desired. From this simple requirement developed a remarkably complex operation and a bewildering variety of technical names—shrouds, ratlines, yards, topgallants, mizzen—all indicating the makeshift nature of the development of sail. A seaman would adapt a rope or piece of canvas for a particular purpose; it would work, and a name would be required for it. The dates in which the various names entered common speech is a good indication of the growth of the full-rigged ship. 'Mizen' identified the aftermost mast of a three-masted vessel in 1420 and was applied to the sail in 1465. 'Top-gallant' came into use in 1514: 'it made a gallant show in comparison with the lower tops'. The term 'shrouds', indicating the ropes which relieved the strain on the mast, was in use from the earliest days of sail, but the term 'ratlines' for the ropes, which linked them on a full-rigged ship and acted as a ladder, came into use only in 1481. Later, when rigging became a more exact science, ships were classified according to their rig, but during the fifteenth and sixteenth centuries the classification was by hull and size. The unit of the ton was used, referring to the carrying capacity of a ship, usually in terms of wine, grain, salt or oil. But the size of the ton itself varied widely, so that a Spanish, Venetian, or English seaman would give the tonnage of the same ship over a wide range.

This was essentially the age of experiment. A shipmaster would modify his vessel; if successful, others would follow and a new class of vessel appear. There were therefore probably scores of classes with only a few vessels in each. But by the end of the fifteenth century two main classes can be distinguished from which all others descended, the caravel and the ship proper. The caravel (8) was a Portuguese contribution, a direct descendant of the lateen-rigged Mediterranean craft. Unlike the early northern full-rigged ship, with a beam nearly half its length, the caravel's beam was rarely more than a quarter. It had only one deck, or even merely half a deck, but in spite of its comparative fragility some of the longest voyages were undertaken in it. It was used to explore the African coast, and two of the three vessels in Columbus' first fleet were of this class. The ship, or *nao*, which came later, was distinguished by its high poop and forecastle. It had been

8   A caravel: from a presumed model of Columbus' *Santa Maria*

the practice during the Middle Ages to equip ships with wooden castles, placed fore and aft and usually manned by archers. At first they were made to be dismantled but later became an integral part of the ship, and in the carrack, the great merchantman of a 1,000 tons or even more, the aftercastle achieved its largest size, seven or eight decks high. At about the same time as the carrack, the fighting ship known as the galleon came into existence. Originally, guns were carried in the castles but between 1500 and 1514 they were placed below decks, firing through gunports; there they remained until the sailing ship as a war vessel passed from history. The galleon was smaller and handier than the towering carrack and in it the forecastle disappeared, giving the craft a clean, raking line (9).

SEAMEN

A ship at sea is even today a world of its own—in spite of virtually instantaneous radio communication. In the days of the great voyages this isolation and sense of community was heightened by the smallness of ship and crew. Rarely did these early vessels achieve 100 feet in length and the number of their crew varied from forty to fifty. The captain was not the god-like figure of absolute authority that he later became; his crew were gathered together in the name of profit and he himself was as ignorant of the perils ahead as any of them. The discipline on a ship wandering in unknown parts of the world, months or even years away from its home base, could be maintained only by a tacit majority verdict. When a great storm threatened to destroy Columbus' ship just a few days before the ending of the triumphant First Voyage, the Admiral ordered that lots should be drawn for one of their number to go on pilgrimage should they survive. He himself took part in the drawing of lots—and the marked bean fell to him. He made the vow, placed his trust in God but continued to act as a prudent seaman, enclosing an account of the voyage in a wooden barrel and throwing it into the sea so that it might survive if they yet foundered.

9 A galleon

The survival of the ship depended upon this sense of unity. Each member of the crew had to be capable of undertaking almost any task—repairing a sail, making a rudder, cooking, splicing, even forging metal parts. Gradually, however, specialised craftsmen began to appear—among them the caulker, the bos'n, the cooper, steward, and carpenter. The caulker's task was the vital one of ensuring that the ship, a moving structure of separate wooden planks, both held together and kept out the water. Oakum was the material used to render seams watertight; it was a loose fibre obtained by picking old ropes and, hammered into a seam, it would swell upon contact with water. Later, the picking of oakum figured largely in prisons and workhouses but in the early days it was yet another task to fill the scanty leisure hours on board. To the bos'n fell the responsibility of maintaining and operating the scores of ropes and sails; working ship was a complex task which required many hands simultaneously, and gradually the bos'n began to figure as a disciplinary officer. The cooper maintained the innumerable casks in which food and water were carried, while the steward, among other duties, trained and supervised the young apprentices. These boys had a duty as important as any on board, for they turned the hour-glass at each half-hour of the watch, accompanying the act with a ritual chant. Much depended upon the alertness of the boy, for once the glass had been turned there was no indication as to whether or not it had been turned on time. A lazy boy could be minutes out; even the most conscientious must have frequently

10   Routine duties at sea

turned a moment too soon or too late, so that error in timekeeping accumulated steadily through a voyage.

The living conditions on these small ships were only just tolerable in fine weather. Hot food was the first comfort to be sacrificed with the onset of bad weather. Cooking facilities consisted simply of a shallow metal tray, filled with sand, and protected by two or three loose bricks, upon which a charcoal fire was lit. In bad weather it was impossible to use; these ships did not cut through the waves as do modern craft but rode upon them, faithfully transmitting every motion of the sea. No captain in his senses would allow an open fire to be used on a pitching, rolling vessel of timber. Food consisted of anything which could be pickled or dried: beef or pork pickled in brine, dried or salt fish, dried peas and beans. The basic meal was probably a kind of stew, a meal which could be prepared without waste and in which the foul taste of the water could be disguised. Water was a permanent problem, for it was stored in oaken casks and after a few weeks could be drunk only through utter necessity. Large quantities of wine and vinegar were carried to supplement it. Bread took the form of pancakes or bannocks cooked in the ashes of the fire. It is not surprising that scurvy—the greatest cause of mortality—appeared as voyages grew longer, for the supply of fresh fruit and vegetables which alone could combat it ran out after a few days at sea. The unremitting physical labour at sea made the crew particularly vulnerable; for hours, perhaps days, on end they might be at their posts—high up in the rigging, wrestling with flapping, soaked canvas, fighting the wheel, pumping ship, all to the accompaniment of violent motion. Off watch, there was no provision for drying clothes beyond that provided by the wind. They slept where they could. Until the early sixteenth century there were no portholes, and the crew therefore spent most of the time on the upper deck. Bunks were provided in some ships but most seamen slept upon a straw-stuffed palliasse, covered by their day clothes. Probably the greatest single boon which the discovery of the Americas brought to the common seaman was the hammock, the suspended bed used by the Indians of Brazil. It can be swung in confined areas where it is impossible to lay a bed, and the most violent movements of the ship are transmuted into a rhythmic swaying. A good diet is essential to withstand such rigorous conditions, and it speaks much for the stamina of these seamen that they survived to explore the world. Nevertheless, iron-hard though they were, scurvy made terrible inroads upon them. In Magellan's fleet, all but fifteen men died of the disease; the 'ship of the dead' was no figment of the imagination, but a real horror only too likely to be encountered. Over 200 years were to pass before the disease was conquered.

In spite of the conditions, a shipmaster never lacked crew if his destination was the New World. Men saw their old friends and neighbours come swaggering home in rich dresses, gold clinking in their purse, with tales of the Eldorado beyond the seas. Nuggets of gold were to be found like stones; slaves in abundance were available, so that no European need do a hand's turn of work. So firmly was this view held that the first settlers in the Carribean, finding neither gold nor slaves, preferred to live in semi-starvation, waiting for food-ships from Spain, rather than till the rich soil beneath their feet. The attitude prevailed during the fantastic years of the conquest and rape of Central America, as the gold of Aztec and Inca poured out in a seemingly endless stream. All that a man had to do was to sign on for an uncomfortable voyage, disembark, and he would infallibly become a prince of princes. It was a heady attraction for a poor, hungry and vigorous European.

Chapter II

THE COURT

THE PRINCE

A T the peak of Renaissance society stood the prince, the single, powerful man who, by a combination of political skill and hereditary authority, virtually ruled absolute over his state. It seems a curious contradiction that this period, which stressed, above all, the freedom of the individual, should have accepted the concept of the single ruler. There was good reason for it. In Italy, where the prince achieved his most brilliant and characteristic form, he was born of the fierce and endless tumults between factions in the cities. Despairing of ever finding peace except under the rule of one man, cities deserted the republican ideal, placing power freely in the hands of a leading citizen. Theoretically, that power was merely lent, not given, but once having enjoyed it few men intended to yield it back. Elsewhere in Europe, similar causes were at work in every country which did not possess a strong, central monarchy. Germany most closely resembled Italy in its bewildering jigsaw of states, for Germany, the home of the Emperor who claimed authority over all monarchs, paradoxically had no king of its own. In England, monarch and subject were in rough equilibrium but there was no doubt about who was prince. The French monarchy was absolute but, under the wretched, mad king Charles VI, the first duke of Burgundy was able to establish a state in the 1360s that he and his descendants turned into a near-monarchy, almost wrecking France in the process. The life of the dukedom of Burgundy was brief, for it was drawn back into France after the death of its last effective duke, Charles the Bold, in 1477, but during those one-hundred-odd years it produced a brilliance which even the Italian courts could not outshine. Spain, slowly being welded into a nation, still showed in its structure its medieval pattern of separate kingdoms.

Theoretically, the term 'prince' could be applied to all who held power, whether over thousands or millions, and it is in this sense that Machiavelli and other political writers used the term. Those princes who contributed most to the new society, however, tended to be smaller rather than larger rulers, exerting a social influence out of proportion to their power until their courts were edged off the European stage by the development of the huge, modern nations. Federigo da Montefeltro, whose court at Urbino set a standard in civilised behaviour for 300 years, ruled perhaps 150,000 souls; those over whom the Medici exercised direct control probably did not exceed a quarter of a million. Even the powerful dukes of Burgundy maintained their independence only through the disordered condition of France. In earlier centuries, much of the energies of these princes would have been expended in war, for military victory meant both glory and survival; the Renaissance prince needed less the virtues of courage and military genius than to be versed in the subtle skills of finance and politics, for war now was in the hands of the professionals. His fame depended less upon battle honours than upon the culture of his court, the extent to which he patronised the arts and showed himself capable of conversing with the learned.

The most brilliant of the Renaissance princes were those early members of the house of Medici which dominated Florence for nearly three hundred years. Rarely can a single family have so influenced an entire continent. It was largely through their munificence and taste that there was gathered in the small city of Florence, during the late fifteenth and early sixteenth centuries the band of men who created the Renaissance. The Medici rule in Florence was tempestuous: three times they were thrown out of the city; three times they returned, creating an ever-closer grip upon the constitution. They took much—but they gave more. The ancient republican history of the city came to an end under them but, under them too, the city became the engine-house of the Renaissance. They poured their enormous wealth into the patronage of the arts and sciences. They spent the better part of four million pounds in less than half a century, not merely in adorning their palaces with works of art but also in endowing seats of learning. Cosimo de' Medici, called 'Pater patriae' by a grateful city, displayed the fantastic generosity of the family to the full in 1439 when the Council of Florence met in the city. He made himself the personal host of the scores of dignitaries attending it, among them the Pope, the Emperor of the East and the Patriarch of Constantinople. The conference was an attempt to achieve a working unity between the Church of Rome and the Eastern Church. It failed, but during the five months that it was in Florence it contributed something possibly even greater to Europe. Some of the most learned people of the world were gathered within the confines of the city between March and July of 1439, and outside the deliberations of the Council they found a ready audience in the Florentines, ever hungry for new ideas. Predominant among these scholars were the Greeks whose language provided the key to the sciences which had so long been lost to Europe. Through their influence Cosimo founded the Platonic Academy which his successors cherished.

In 1444 Cosimo began the construction of the first of the Medici palaces. His fellow-citizens protested, thinking it both unfitting and ominous that a so-called private citizen should build upon such a scale. They tried to unseat him but he weathered that particular storm although others were to follow. Later, when the Medici became overlords in law as they were in fact, and took the title of Duke, they built an enormous palace on the far side of the Arno— a sprawling, arrogant building which proclaimed the superior status of the family. But Cosimo's palace, where the Renaissance can be said to have been born, appears more as a private house in its exterior for it fits into the line of the street (*11*). It was the first of the Renaissance palaces, providing the model for scores to come. Medici rule was still far from absolute and the palace still had to discharge the function of a castle where the family could shelter from the rage of their fellows. The ground storey therefore appears solid, almost forbidding, but the upper stories are elegant. The great street door gave on to a little court, graceful and airy, and

11 Palace of the Medici, Florence, which took 20 years to complete

here were placed the statues of *David* and *Judith* which Donatello had been commissioned to produce while the palace was being constructed. The *David* was a work of a kind which had not been seen in Europe for over a thousand years, for it was executed in the round and, like the palace in which it stood, created a precedent for others to follow. *Judith slaying Holofernes* was a favourite allegorical subject among the Italian city-states for it could be applied to any current enemy. Fifty years after its completion, when the Medici palace was sacked and the family driven out, the statue was set up in a public place with an inscription giving warning 'to all who should think to tyrannise over Florence'. The Medici nevertheless came back.

In 1469 Lorenzo de' Medici became head of the family and of the State (*13*). He was only twenty years old at the time and, although bred to responsibility, was vividly aware of the burden he had to bear. 'The second day after my father's death, the principal men of the city and of the State came to our house to condole with us on our loss, and to encourage me to take on the care of the city and of the State as my father and grandfather had done. This proposal being against the instincts of my immature age, and considering that the burden and danger were great, I consented to it unwillingly.' His reason for acceptance was the sound, practical reason of finance which the Medici never quite abandoned. 'I did so in order to protect our friends and property for it fares ill in Florence with any who possesses wealth without any share in the government.' The Florentines thereby gained a leader who combined in his person all the qualities of the rich and diverse period. Financier and poet, statesman and scholar, economist and strategist—it seemed that there was no activity in which he could not excel if he so desired. The consummate political and military skill with which he steered Florence through the dangerous shoals of Italian politics ultimately left no trace, for Florence, with all Italy, became subject to foreigners. It was the manner in which he cherished and directed the new-born arts and learning which left its mark upon Europe. His patronage made heavy inroads even upon the great Medici fortune, but he looked upon himself as a custodian, rather than an owner, of wealth. 'Some would perhaps think it more desirable to have a part of it in their purse but I conceive it to have been spent to the great advantage of the public and am therefore perfectly satisfied.'

The vast library which he amassed became the first true public library in Europe for it was freely available to all. Agents were engaged not only in Europe but in the East with the express purpose of discovering ancient manuscripts. One scholar brought back 200 Greek works, eighty of which had never before been known in Europe. The names of the innumerable artists he encouraged would be a catalogue of the creators of the Renaissance. Botticelli, five years his senior, had shared his childhood home and later worked for him; Leonardo da Vinci owed his appointment to the Milanese court to him; he gave the 15-year-old Michelangelo a home in his palace with a monthly allowance; Verrocchio, Ghirlandajo, Filippino Lippi—so the list could be extended until it included every talented man working in Florence during the brief years of Lorenzo's life. He died at the age of forty-three, but, though no other Medici could equal the versatility of 'Il Magnifico', yet they continued his work. One of them became pope as Leo X and infused into the most powerful court in Europe some of the ideals which Lorenzo had cherished.

Renaissance society, having perforce accepted the single ruler, did not thereby accept him as a natural phenomenon to be endured or adored. His office was analysed, as it had never been before, in an attempt to explain its growth and function, to prepare a blue-print of a piece of political machinery which was to drive Europe for nearly three hundred years. The machinery was 'political' in the fullest sense, for it governed in some degree

12 Diplomacy in action
Detail from Carpaccio's 'St Ursula'

13   Lorenzo de' Medici
From a terracotta bust by Andrea Verrocchio

14   (*overleaf*) Tourney at Nuremberg, 1561
From a painting by J. Ammam

**A RENAISSANCE PRINCE
AND HIS WIFE**

*From paintings by Ercole
Roberti, c. 1480*

16   Ginevra Bentivoglio, daughter
of Alessandro Sforza, Lord of
Pesaro

15   Giovanni il Bentivoglio,
Lord of Bologna

every aspect of the lives of men
gathered together in communities,
decreeing how they should be judged,
how they should earn their bread, re-
fresh their minds and bodies, protect
themselves from enemies within and
without the State. Two books appeared in the early years of the
sixteenth century which placed the
prince and his court under the
microscope, *The Prince* by Niccolo
Machiavelli (*17*) and *The Courtier*
by Baldassare Castiglione. They
appeared within four years of each
other, in 1528 and 1532 respectively,
but both had been written, quite

17 Niccolo Machiavelli
*After the portrait by Santi di
Tito*

independently, many years before—testimony to the fact that the
phenomenon of the prince was beginning to engage European
attention. Machiavelli's intention was to dissect the mechanics of
statecraft in terms of its effectiveness. Morality was irrelevant:
if a strategy worked, it was good; if it failed, it was bad. There
have been few writers so grossly misjudged as this Florentine
republican who produced the classic textbook for the practice of
tyranny. It is as though a doctor, having diagnosed a disease, were
to be accused of inventing it. Machiavelli was well aware of the
construction likely to be placed upon his work and went out of his
way to stress that this was the picture of things as they were—that,
given that the prince was necessary in civil life, then it was best
that he should learn how to conduct himself in the most perilous
craft in the world. He should indeed be a wise and virtuous man,
but 'the manner in which men now live is so different from the
manner in which they should live that he who deviates from the
common course of practice and endeavours to act as duty dictates,
necessarily ensures his own destruction'. Every man has a price,
every seemingly disinterested action can be shown to be rooted in
self-interest. A prince should keep his word—but few successful
men actually do so. Is it better for a prince to be loved or feared?
It depends, Machiavelli replies; circumstances alter cases but, on
the whole, it is safer to be feared, for most men are fickle and
timid and will abandon in the hour of need those who have

favoured them and have no other call upon them than the claims of gratitude. A prince as a commander of troops should always be feared, never worrying about a reputation for cruelty, for this was the only possible way to keep cruel men in order. It was a jaundiced view of the world; none knew better than Machiavelli that men could, and did, die for no other price than love of their country. But such love presupposed freedom; where there was no longer freedom the only incentives were self-interest or fear.

Machiavelli's prince was the first among men but was still a man; the Latin mind declined to invest him with that tinge of divinity which, in the north, came to infuse the idea. In Burgundy, the concept of the duke as being the personification of the State, and therefore as being something greater than a common man, was erected into a principle and a ritual. All the trappings of adoration, more commonly reserved for the worship of God, were his. Religious texts which spoke of the Trinity were freely applied to his comings and goings. After certain festivities in Arras, le Clerc wrote: 'If God were to descend from heaven I doubt if they could do him greater honour than was made to the duke.' Another remarked of the enthusiasm shown in the streets, 'It seemed as though they had God himself by the feet'. The most precious metals were considered only just good enough to touch his sacred flesh, be viewed by his holy eyes. The attendance at table upon him echoed the ritual of the Holy Mass; his very cup-bearer was seen as the priest who, in another church, elevated the chalice. Even as at the altar, the napkin with which the duke dried his hands was kissed as it was passed from courtier to courtier. The torches which lit his way to table were kissed, as were the handles of the knives placed before him. Such adulation would have astonished the Italians. Lorenzo de' Medici, popular and competent though he was, came under heavy and sustained criticisms for his pretensions: 'He did not want to be equalled or imitated even in verses or games or exercises and turned angrily on any one who did so.' No one would have dared even attempt to be the equal of a duke of Burgundy. The excess was to bring its reaction: a king of England lost his head through too much devotion to the Divine Right and the monarchy of France ultimately collapsed in bloody ruin.

THE COURTIER

Machiavelli's *Prince* was a cold exercise in logic; Castiglione's

Courtier was a warm, living portrait of the ideal man. 'I do not wonder that you were able to depict the perfect courtier', a friend wrote to him, 'for you had only to hold a mirror before you and set down what you saw there.' The graceful compliment was essentially true for Castiglione possessed most of the qualities he praised: piety, loyalty, courage, an easy learning and wit. Indeed, his life was almost a demonstration of Machiavelli's opinion that a virtuous man was at a disadvantage. As envoy between Pope Clement VII and the Emperor Charles V during the perilous days which culminated in the Sack of Rome in 1527, he was deluded by both, failed in his mission and died a discredited man. The Emperor, who so sorely tried him, said sadly, 'I tell you, one of the finest gentlemen in the world is dead'. Castiglione would have been proud of the epitaph and history, too, remembers him, not as diplomat but as gentleman.

The Courtier was the outcome of four brief years spent at the little court of Urbino. Afterwards, Castiglione was to mix with the truly great and powerful. As representative of the duke at the Papal Court, he came into intimate contact with Raphael, Michelangelo, Bembo; later he was Apostolic Nuncio to the Emperor's court. But always he looked back with nostalgia to the little court set among the hills of the northern Marches. He left Urbino in 1508, but for twenty years thereafter he lovingly polished and re-polished his account of a civilised society, creating a monument to his own Golden Age. The duchy of Urbino owed its foundation to Federigo da Montefeltro, a professional soldier who yet managed to create a court in which the new humanist values were dazzlingly embodied. Piero della Francesca's portrait of him shows a man in whom strength is combined with tolerance (*18*), who would be surprised by nothing, expected nothing and was well able to defend his own

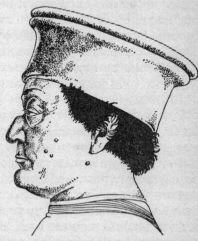

18   Federigo da Montefeltro, Duke of Urbino

After the portrait by Piero della Francesca

rights. The hooded eyes are deceptively sleepy; the firm mouth will smile easily; the great, broken nose and jutting chin thrust aggressively forward. He was a man who made a fortune from soldiering, played off his enemies one against the other and so kept inviolate the 400-odd hill villages and towns which acknowledged him as prince. But he was also a man who, in childhood, had been schooled by Vittorino da Feltre, the greatest humanist teacher in Europe, who infused in his pupils the new view of man. The great library at Urbino was Federigo's work. 'He alone had a mind to do what had not been done for a thousand years and more; that is, to create the finest library since ancient times.' Not for him was the common product of the new printing press; he employed thirty or forty scribes so that all his books should be 'written with the pen, not one printed, that it might not be disgraced thereby'.

In 1450 he began the construction of the palace(19) which Castiglione knew and which attracted travellers on the Grand Tour long after the brief life of the duchy had passed. 'It seemed not a palace but a city in the form of a palace', Castiglione affirmed, 'and [he] furnished it not only with what is customary such as silver vases, wall hangings of the richest cloth of gold, silk and other like things but for ornament he added countless ancient statues of marble and bronze, rare paintings . . .' In this twofold role, admirer of ancient art and patron of modern painters, Federigo was essentially of the Renaissance. He died in 1482 and the dukedom passed to his son, Guidobaldo, who maintained the intellectual atmosphere of the court although he proved himself unable to hold back the militant world outside. It was his court which Castiglione described in the process of building up the portrait of the courtier. It is the picture of a group of brilliant minds, familiar with each other and therefore at ease, who have turned aside briefly from the cares of state and seek refreshment in conversation. There are feasts and entertainments of wide variety; during the day the members go about their business but each evening they meet again, under the presidency of the duchess (for the duke is grievously afflicted by gout and retires early). They talk into the small hours, pursuing each topic informally but with sobriety and order—and merriment too—fashioning between themselves the perfect man. So vividly did the memory stay with Castiglione that he could describe the end of one of these sessions with the poignancy of a paradise lost.

19 Courtyard of Federigo da Montefeltro's Palace at Urbino

Then every man rose to his feet ... and not one of them felt any heaviness of sleep. When the windows were open then upon the side of the Palace that looks towards Mount Catri, they saw already risen in the east, a fair morning, rose coloured, and all stars gone save only Venus, from which seemed to blow a sweet blast that, filling the air with biting cold, began to quicken the notes of the pretty birds among the hushing woods of the hills nearby. Then they all, taking their leave with reverence of the Duchess, departed toward their lodging without torch, the light of day sufficing.

After Castiglione's day, the image of the courtier suffered a decline, becoming either the image of a fop or an intriguing social climber; even the Italian feminine of the word—'*la cortegiana*' or courtesan—became a synonym for a high-class harlot. But for Castiglione, the courtier was the cream of civilised society. He did not have to be nobly born; admittedly, he usually was, for only those born into the upper classes had the leisure or the opportunities to practise the arts, but this recognition that 'courtesy' was a quality of mind, and not of class, went far to explain the wide influence of the book. The courtier must be able to acquit himself in all manly exercises—wrestling, running, riding, but should be equally at home with literature, able to speak several languages, play musical instruments, write elegant verse (*20*). But everything should be done with a casual air so that his conversation, though sensible, was sprightly; he was even enjoined to study the form and nature of jokes. In love, he was to be discreet and honourable; in war, courageous but magnanimous. Above all, he was to be a man of his word, loyal to his prince, generous to his servants. He was altogether far removed from that other

20 'The Garden of Love'

ideal man, the knight, with his fantastic code of personal honour. In modern language, Castiglione's courtier would be described as a well-educated, 'decent' man, with a strong code of personal morals but tolerant of the weakness of others. It was an ideal by which most men probably measured their lapses, for the standard demanded was high. But that the book filled a void is well shown by the speed with which it entered other languages and how long it maintained its influence. It was translated into French in 1537, into Spanish in 1540, into English in 1561, and, 200 years after Urbino ceased to exist as a state, Samuel Johnson gave his benediction to the book which enshrined its memory. 'The best book that ever was written upon good breeding, Il Cortegiano, by Castiglione, grew up at the little court of Urbino and you should read it.'

THE KNIGHT

Chivalry had long since abandoned its early, noble ideals which saw the metal-clad, mounted man as defender of the defenceless, enemy of the enemies of Christ. The great military orders had come into being during the endless attempts to win back the Holy Places from the Saracen and formed a kind of permanent, international army. But as the prospect of defeating the Saracen waned, and the Crusades died, the consecrated nature of knighthood disappeared. Until the late fifteenth century, the knight still had a military task to discharge for he and his heavily armed fellows formed the core of an army. But the special aura still clung to him, forbidding him to earn his keep by any other way but his sword; if he lacked private means, then the only source of income open to him was a pension from his prince and booty from war. On the battlefield, his rigid code of conduct placed him at a disadvantage when faced with the new professionals. The English, less tied to the ideal of knighthood, less class-conscious, evolved a highly effective army which drew upon the skills of common men. The French for long clung to the idea of war as being a species of game conducted between equals—with results such as Crécy, Poitiers and Agincourt. But, even as the military and Christian values of the knight declined, his outward pageantries grew ever more splendid, the shadow increasing as the substance lessened.

The social splendour of the knight was displayed at the tourney, the war-game which was once his training ground and was now his stage. Many a knight bankrupted himself in order to appear in fitting state; even if he did not directly squander his sustenance on splendid armour and horses and reckless largesse, his domestic affairs deteriorated as he wandered from tourney to tourney. There had been many attempts to control this passion; some monarchs forbade their knights to attend tourneys on pain of fine or even death, others licensed tourneys only for specific times and places. The monarch's interest arose less from the fact that his knights were impoverishing themselves, than that he was deprived of their services during their endless touring of Europe in search of honour. The proclaimed ambition of the Burgundian cavalier, Jacques de Lalaing, was to fight thirty times in the lists before his thirtieth year, in addition to honours gained during normal military service. He died at the age of thirty-two—killed by a cannon-ball; it was an appropriate death, for the cannon consigned the armoured knight into oblivion as a soldier.

It was probably because the element of danger was thus taken out of the profession of chivalry that there occurred an extraordinary increase in the number of knights from the late fourteenth century onwards. The passion for titles of knighthood ran through republics and monarchies alike, affecting legitimate holders of ancient names as well as upstart merchants anxious to find a place in society. The pretensions became a target for scorn. Italy, ahead in this as in most other activities, began the debunking of the corrupted ideal; Spain finished it with Cervantes' immortal 'Knight of the Sorrowful Countenance' who presented in his doleful person all that was ludicrous in knight-errantry. Particular scorn was directed at the 'holiday cavaliers', those honest tradesmen who abandoned their sober tasks to waste time and money on tournaments. The Florentine novelist Sachetti pilloried one such, an elderly lawyer who, on a hired horse, went off to tourneys whenever he could until the day a practical joker placed a thistle under his horse's tail. The horse bolted, the lawyer's horsemanship was shown up for what it was, and, bruised, dishevelled and frightened, he was eventually deposited at the feet of his scolding wife before his jeering fellow-citizens. Most Italian cities provided stiff penalties for those who assumed arms without legal justification, but it had little effect. In Bourges, in France, one of the king's ministers gave a tournament of donkeys; a prince of Milan knighted the victor in a brawl and then, contemptuously, did the same for the loser. But the mockery of thoughtful men and the threats of governments were alike in vain; the tourney continued to flourish.

The actual tourney was always a rough, frequently a dangerous, and sometimes a fatal sport. It could not be otherwise when half a ton of metal-clad horse and man crashed into

21 The tourney: the knight on the far side of the tilt has been swept from the saddle

another at a combined speed of perhaps 30 miles an hour. Few lances could stand the impact and it was a common practice to measure a man's prowess by the number of lances he had shivered against an opponent. In the sixteenth century, some of the element of danger was removed by the erection of a tilt, a long barrier which separated the charging knights so that only a glancing blow was delivered (21). But the combat itself was, in any case, giving ground to the splendid irrelevancies which preceded and followed it. Hundreds, perhaps thousands, of people were attracted to a tournament who had neither desire nor intention of risking their necks (14). They gathered in the spirit of any crowd gathering for any festival: to show off their clothes, to drink, eat, pursue a love affair. Deplorable though it might seem to the dedicated knight, who desired only the chance to hammer another metal-clad man with metal, the tournament became a set-piece resembling a stage show. The famous tournament of the Tree of Gold, held in Bruges in 1468, established a glittering precedent. Each of the champions created a pageant for himself to mark his entry into the arena. One even appeared in a complete castle on wheels but most contented themselves with fables on the theme of the knight enslaved by love. Elaborate banquets marked the end of each day, their expense being borne by the Duke of Burgundy—and ultimately by his subjects.

The Tree of Gold was probably the last of the great tournaments.

Half a century later, Europe was dazzled by the prodigal splendour of the Field of the Cloth of Gold but there, though tourneys ran every day, they lacked the curious dedication of the Burgundians. In June 1559, Henry II of France was killed in the tournament of Vosges. He had already held two courses against two different knights; in the third course against a young knight, both lances were broken. Reluctant to allow a young man the honour of having broken a lance against the king of France, Henry insisted that another course should be run. The trumpeters, who usually kept up a continuous fanfare throughout a course, fell silent as though from presentiment and it was in a total hush that the last charge took place. Again both lances were broken, the horsemen continued past each other but the splintered lance of the young knight struck the King beneath his visor. He died ten days later. The tournament of Vosges was the last ever held in that court of France which, of all others, had been the nourisher of chivalry.

SOCIAL LIFE

There was a very wide range in the luxuries or even the ordinary necessities of life available in the different courts of Europe. The north, in general, lagged far behind the south not merely in matters of etiquette and ornament but in ordinary hygiene. As late as 1608 the dining fork was still an object of curiosity in England. 'This form of feeding, I understand, is generally used in all places in Italy . . . because the Italian cannot by any means endure to have his dish touched with his fingers, seeing that all men's fingers are not alike clean.' In 1568 Thomas Sackville, an English lord, protested at being obliged to entertain a cardinal, giving a woeful picture of life in his particular princely establishment. He had no precious plate at all; the glasses he did possess were rejected by the king's agents as being too base; his napery, too, was sneered at: 'they desired damask and I had nothing but plain linen'. He had only one spare bed, which the cardinal occupied; in order to get a bed for the bishop his wife's waiting women had to sleep on the floor. He himself had to loan his basin and ewer to the cardinal and, in consequence, was obliged to go unwashed. All this compares sadly with the experience of an ordinary English gentleman who was entertained in Salerno by an Italian marquis. His chamber was hung in cloth of gold and velvet; he and his companion had a bed each, the one covered with silver cloth, the other velvet; pillows, bolsters and sheets were all beautifully embroidered —and clean. The lack of cleanliness was one of the things the Italian noticed when he ventured beyond the Alps. A young Italian nobleman, Massimiano Sforza, educated in Germany, picked up the most filthy habits; neither the ridicule of his male friends nor the pleadings of women could induce him to change his underwear. Henry VIII of England was reputed never to have seen his naked feet from one year's end to the next. In a society where most went unwashed, few would complain of, or even notice, the prevailing odour; nevertheless, the wide use of perfumes argues that the threshold of tolerance was frequently exceeded. Perfumes were used not merely for the body but for objects which passed from hand to hand; the gift of a bouquet of flowers had a very real value, as well as a symbolic meaning.

The heavy stuffs and rich embroidery of contemporary costume must have contributed largely to the problems of personal hygiene. Medieval costume had been comparatively simple. There were naturally variants based on personal taste and wealth but essentially it had consisted of the flowing robe of single colour. But with the fifteenth and sixteenth centuries there burst upon the world a peacock blaze of colour and a fantastic distortion of form. Not content with the richness and heaviness of brocades and velvets, the rich covered these fabrics with pearls, gold embroidery and precious stones so thickly placed together that the fabric was not visible. Primary colours were favoured both as single colour and in contrast with one another. In the opening years of the sixteenth century the bizarre fashion of parti-colour swept through Europe (22). It was a logical development from the fashion of using clashing colours for different garments. Sections of the same costume would be in different

22 Parti-colour costume

53

colours, the leg of one hose red, the other green; a sleeve in purple, another in orange, the body of the garment itself being in a third colour. Each person of fashion was his or her own designer, and in any one assembly would appear a wide and wild variety of dress. Fashions changed with a rapidity which had been unknown before. A London chronicler, writing in the age of Elizabeth I, remarked: 'Forty years ago there were not 12 haberdashers in London who sold fancy caps, glasses, swords, daggers, girdles; now, from the Tower to Westminster, every street is full of them and their shops glitter and shine of glass.' In every country, moralists deplored the decline from the standards of the past, the aping of the fashions of other countries.

23   Costume of an English nobleman, *c.* 1600

Behold a most accomplished cavalier,
That the world's ape of Fashion doth appear.
Walking the streets his humours to disclose,
In the French doublet and the German hose,
The muff cloak, Spanish hat, Toledo blade,
Italian ruff, a shoe right Flemish made.

There was no garment or part of a garment which was not affected by the feverish desire for originality; to attempt to catalogue the changes would be to attempt to pin down a fashion which altered even as it was being accepted. The male costume consisted basically of doublet and hose, the former a close-fitting garment somewhat resembling a modern waistcoat, the latter, introduced as stockings, ended as breeches or trousers (*23, 30*). But scores of variations were played upon this basic theme. Sleeves became detachable, each costing a small fortune; the modest inch or so of white linen at the neck developed into the monstrous cartwheel ruff; the hose developed into the trunk-hose, bombasted or padded out to enormous extent. Slashing appeared, one of the few fashions which moved upward in society for it was first adopted by Swiss mercenaries. The material of doublet and hose was literally slashed with thousands of cuts, showing a different coloured material underneath. The Germans

24   French court costume, *c.* 1555
After a portrait of Catherine de' Medici

carried this to extremes, developing the incredibly baggy breeches which employed 20 yards or more of material falling in loose strips from hip to knee. Women were no less extravagant, managing to evolve a costume which exposed most of the bosom while confining the rest of the body in a kind of cage. Their court portraits show them posed in an almost inhuman stiffness, the waist pinched in as close to vanishing point as possible, the skirt swelling out like a tent (24). The henin—the yard-high head-dress —still persisted. In its most extravagant form a heavy veil descended from its topmost peak to trail on the ground. In some palaces, doors had actually to be heightened to allow the fashionable lady to pass through.

The taste for extravagant dress spread downwards through society; the country yokel, abandoning his sober homespun for cheap finery, was a stock figure of fun (25). 'Today one cannot tell

25 Caricature of Elizabethan fashions

potboy from lord, serving wench from lady', was a common complaint. There was some truth in it for with the rise of a wealthy middle class and a slight increase in the standards of the poor, swaggering in fine clothes was no longer the absolute privilege of any one class. In an attempt to preserve social distinctions, sumptuary laws were revived; they prescribed, minutely, what could and could not be worn by various classes. Elizabeth of England forbade the ruff and farthingale for the common; in France, brocades of gold and silver were reserved for those of the royal blood; in Florence, ordinary women were forbidden the use of various kinds of fur, various shapes of, and materials for, buttons. The laws were no sooner passed than they fell into disrepute, were enacted again with other variations of prohibitions and penalties—and were again ignored. Purse alone could act as restraint.

The recreations of the court very much reflected the cast of mind of the prince. The sober enjoyment of intellectual discussion, which Castiglione remembered as being essentially a part of Urbino, was by no means general. The Germans took their pleasures boisterously; drinking was the national art and they favoured an uproarious style of dancing which brought the censure of the sober. Yet Montaigne, connoisseur of good manners, was impressed with the affectionate but decorous dancing he saw in Augsburg. 'The gentleman took the lady's hand, kissed it and placed his hand on her shoulder and holding her closely so that they were cheek to cheek. The lady placed a hand on his shoulder and in this way they circled round the room. The menfolk have their own seats quite apart from the ladies and do not care to mix with them.' The introduction of women into court festivals was a marked feature and one which probably went far to tone down the earlier extravagances (26). The courtesan had arrived—the beautiful, accomplished woman who, for a fee, would grace any occasion. Many of them were widely educated, able to hold their own in any conversation, and frequently kept their own courts where the great of society could find refreshment and distraction from affairs of state among their own kind. The courtesan did not displace, but supplemented the wife. Marriage continued to be by arrangement; no sensible family would allow the possession of valuable lands and property to be jeopardised by casual alliances. The young noble, for his part, having performed his duty by a marriage alliance with someone he may have never met before, saw no reason why he should not find his pleasures elsewhere. Society agreed with him. Nevertheless, the slightly better education which women were receiving enabled them to play a more active part in society, and the wife stepped out of the background she had long occupied.

The serving of an elaborate meal in order to honour a distinguished guest or entertain a household is an abiding and universal custom. The Renaissance court took the custom, embellished it, and made of it an affair which was more appropriate to the stage than the dining-room (27). Indeed, the twin arts of ballet and opera were probably born of the 'table decorations', which made of the meal itself a mere by-product. The elaboration probably originated in Italy, but again it was the court of

26   Masquerade at the court of the Emperor

27   Banquet at a French court

Burgundy which staged feasts to scandalise the moral and delight the worldly. The most splendid of these was the Feast of the Pheasant of 1454. Constantinople had fallen to the Turks the year before and the Feast was designed to spark off the last Crusade. The Crusade never took place, and there is a curious irony in this Feast of the Pheasant, which ushered in the Renaissance while supposedly reviving a dream of the Middle Ages.

The details of the Feast had been kept a close secret until, after three days of minor banqueting, the privileged were ushered into the great Hotel de la Salle. It was January and the hall was ablaze with light from innumerable candles and torches; the servants were in a sober livery of grey and black, acting as a foil to the gold and scarlet, satins, velvets and brocades of the guests. There were three tables, covered with silk damask, each of enormous size for they were also to act as stage. Long before the actual banquet commenced, the diners strolled round what can only be described as sideshows. Upon the duke's table was a model church, complete with belfry, and containing four musicians. A complete, rigged ship, with a working crew, was upon the same table together with a complex fountain of glass and precious stones. A great pie

58

28   Renaissance Palace
Detail from Albrecht Altdorfer's 'Susanna Bathing', 1526

29 Sixteenth-century noblewoman
From a drawing by Hans Holbein, 1527

30 English courtier of 1602
From a portrait of Sir Walter Raleigh

THE ELABORATION OF COSTUME

held twenty-eight musicians; clockwork animals prowled through exquisitely formed jungles; living people enacted tableaux of proverbs. During the banquet, the food was lowered from the ceiling but probably few were able uninterruptedly to enjoy a single course. Sixteen 'interludes' followed: jugglers, singers, acrobats, even a falcon hunt with living birds took place on the floor of the hall. An elaborate mystery play, the Story of Jason, with fire-breathing bulls, dragons, and armed men was enacted upon a proper stage. But interludes and mystery alike were but a prelude to the grand set piece, the plea of Constantinople for aid. A giant, dressed as a Saracen, entered leading an elephant on whose back was a woman dressed in mourning. She was the Church, come to plead for the Duke's aid for her lost city and, after a dirge, a herald came on with a live pheasant in his hands. It had long been a custom for knights to pledge an irrevocable oath while eating of some bird deemed noble—peacock, heron or pheasant. The symbolism was modified upon this occasion and the oath to redeem Constantinople was taken upon the living bird which was afterwards released. The solemn proceedings then ended with a ball.

Chess and dice, archery and tennis, cards, football, singing and gambling—all these were the informal amusements of the court (*31*). But the sport which most clearly proclaimed aristocracy was hunting (*32*). Even the most enlightened prince thought nothing of retaining large tracts of country for his especial use; the subjects of a brutal

31 Chess: from a Florentine treatise on the game, written in 1493

32 The prince hunts with his court

prince had cause to curse the survival of this primeval activity. In order to protect game for their sport, princes enacted the most rigorous laws, even visiting the extreme penalty of death upon the man who illegally killed protected game. Both birds and animals flourished unchecked, destroying or devouring far more of the growing crops than were destroyed by the hunt itself. The prince did not hunt alone: he might decide to spend days in some favoured part of the country, bringing with him a great entourage and conducting affairs of state in the field. Nights of feasting and dancing followed the energetic days and here, perhaps, the great social contrast of the time was most pointed. Not far from the hunting lodge, ablaze with light, merry with song, would be the tumbledown hovel of the peasant from whom, ultimately, came the wealth for this display.

Chapter III

THE MERCHANT

THERE was little outwardly to distinguish the wealthy merchant from the prince. Dressed in furs and silks, his house richly furnished and decorated with a newly purchased coat of arms, directly controlling the lives of hundreds or even thousands of men, he had arrived as a new force in society. Some merchants became princes in fact: the court of the Medici was founded firmly on trade and finance; others, like the Fuggers of Augsburg, preferred the reality without the trappings of power, making and unmaking princes as part of their financial activities. The merchants of the Hanseatic League ruled like despots in dozens of cities scattered about Europe. Once, the kings of Europe had contemptuously demanded aid of the despised money-lender, repaying or not as they chose. Now the money-lender, transformed into the merchant and the banker, was at the council table dictating policy.

Medieval trade had been essentially inter-urban, merchants transporting goods from one city of Europe to another, acting as a kind of bloodstream for the circulation of wealth. The feudal system had greatly limited trade, since there was little incentive for the serf, as worker, to produce more than was required for his own and his lord's consumption. Localities were self-contained, each producing its own necessities, the products of the blacksmith, the farmer, the wheelwright travelling only a few miles from their place of production. Wheat was one of the few bulk commodities of low price in which the merchant dealt; he could always count upon famine conditions, in at least one part of Europe, giving him handsome return for his outlay. He had to bear in mind the difficulty and cost of transport; all goods were carried overland by pack-animals, the cost of which was almost four times as great as water-transport. Trade had therefore followed the great rivers of Europe, and humble depots along the banks of the Rhine, the Rhône, the Po developed into rich and powerful cities. They

33 Loading merchandise at Hamburg in 1487

provided safety, and a means of trading; in return they took a large slice of profits in the form of various custom tolls.

But the carrying capacity of rivercraft, though far greater than that of animals, was still limited; merchants found that the highest returns were brought by articles of small bulk and high intrinsic value —silk, saffron, spices from the East, wax from the 'honey trees' of Russia, alum from the Balkans. The fact that Europe was a Christian continent, with innumerable days throughout the year in which meat-eating was forbidden, resulted in a flourishing trade of fish, mostly herrings, from the north. The powerful Hansa owed its origins to this humble source. Wine travelled from south to north; wool circulated between sheep-farm and weaver, from weaver to tailor, creating enormous fortunes for individuals, cities and whole countries. The luxury trade from the East was firmly in the hands of Genoese and Venetians. The silks which clothed the nobles, the pearls which glowed upon the bosoms of their ladies, the spices which enlivened their monotonous diet had come an incredible journey by land and sea. India was the great market of the East; there, Arabs loaded silks and pepper, pearls and muslin, and sailed up the Persian Gulf to Ormuz. The goods were taken thence by caravan to Baghdad, meeting place of East and West. A Baghdad merchant, describing his activities, gave a picture of the enormous spider's web of commerce which the city controlled: 'I take the sulphur of Persia to China, Chinese porcelain to Greece,

Greek brocades to Aleppo, Aleppo glass to Yemen and Yemen fabrics to Persia.' Goods for the West went from Baghdad to Tyre or Antioch, where Venetian and Genoese galleys were waiting to transport them to Europe.

The exotic goods of the East and the more humdrum goods of Europe met at last in one of the great fairs which were scattered over the Continent. The most important were probably those located in Flanders—over thirty 'nations' were registered in Bruges alone—and much of the later wealth of the Low Countries sprang from this fact. But all countries had certain cities where fairs were held: Champagne and Brie in France; Stourbridge and Smithfield in England; Seville in Spain; Leipzig in Germany; and, perhaps the greatest of all, Nijni Novgorod in Russia. The larger fairs appeared as temporary cities, with streets of booths allocated to specific trades: here leather and cloth, there precious fabrics—brocades, silks, velvets; elsewhere spices, wines, foodstuffs. An important figure was the money-changer; every currency in Europe would be in circulation and a merchant would naturally wish to take away his profit in the currency of his own land. At the end of the fair, a period was allowed for the settling of accounts. Merchants were held communally responsible for the credit of fellow-countrymen so that the debts of a defaulting Venetian, for example, would have to be paid by the entire Venetian 'nation' at the following fair. The system ensured a high standard of probity.

34　Travelling players at a carnival

Fairs brought considerable colour and gaiety into the lives of townsfolk, for, wherever crowds with money to spend are gathered together, there come a whole itinerant class to charm that money from them. Jugglers, players, singers, astrologers, glib-tongued men with universal nostrums, thundering friars with messages of damnation, conjurors, strong men, thieves, all made their appearance. There was usually a strong committee controlling the fair, but licences could be obtained and if they were denied—then the money to be made outweighed the penalties for unlicensed activities. Ultimately, this element of entertainment took over from the commercial, but even today specialised fairs continue throughout Europe. Apart from their economic and entertainment value, fairs discharged a considerable social function in acting as a sounding-board of European opinion. Through them, intelligent men from all parts of the Continent met regularly and, their work completed, would naturally fall to exchanging news and opinions about this and that state of society. It was in this informal manner that much of the values of Renaissance Italy entered Europe.

The fair was born of the nomadic nature of medieval trade, and continued in strength long after the more static nature of modern buying and selling was established. But the great merchant of the Renaissance formed his own focal point to which lesser men were attracted; his agents might attend fairs, but he himself remained in his counting house. It was the flood of gold from the New World which was a major factor in the creation of the powerful new class of merchant. Gold, unlike goods, does not deteriorate or lessen in value if hoarded; unlike land, it can be put in a place of safety. The modern merchant could therefore build up capital almost independent of the society in which he found himself, unlike his predecessors whose capital was tied up in perishable goods or came from vulnerable estates. A Fugger agent, making a routine report about the arrival of a Spanish gold fleet in September 1583, stated that it was carrying some 15 million ducats of gold. The fleet had been obliged to unload a million in Havana, so heavily were the ships laden. He ended his report with the remark, 'This is a pretty penny which will give new life to commerce'. For many centuries, Europe's limited supply of gold had been trickling out to the East to purchase those Oriental luxuries whose possession was a hallmark of success. By the middle of the fifteenth century the total supply was probably at the lowest it had ever been.

THE MERCHANT

The first expeditions to the New World yielded little but, just eleven years after Columbus' landfall, the first large consignment of gold was sent back to Europe. Thereafter, as the conquistadores hacked their way through Mexico, gold and silver in astounding quantities entered European coffers so that the supply of bullion was probably increased fivefold during the century. Spain, who at the beginning controlled most of this flood, was almost ruined by it. Gold could buy anything—so everything was bought, at the expense of the development of local industries and crafts. Aztec gold proved to be fairy gold for the ordinary Spaniard.

But the merchant waxed ever richer, particularly as the ancient ban upon usury lost its force. From the earliest days of the Church it was held that money was a dead thing, and that any attempt to make a dead thing reproduce itself was unnatural, an offence against the laws of God and man. Strictly, the ban was aimed at money-lending, an odious profession in the eyes of most people, not least those who had recourse to it. In the main square of every city was to be seen the money-lender's little booth, furnished with a table, much-used ledger and cash-box (35). To it came the improvident and the unfortunate, the spendthrift young man and the hard-working farmer whose crops had failed that year and who must needs have gold to feed his family until spring. Money was available to all—at a price: 20, 30, 40 per cent, whatever the money-lender deemed could be extracted. The borrower, in return, if he could not offer

35 The money-lender and his wife
After a painting by Quentin Matsys

36   Venice in 1485, showing ship-building and a varie

the security of a wealthy friend, left a pledge. Governments in most countries attempted to control the nature of pledges, forbidding the acceptance of working men's tools as a pawn; usually, a garment or household implement was offered. The trade being forbidden to Christians, it fell largely into the hands of the Jews who were denied most other means of livelihood. The identification of this trade with the Jews was probably the greatest single source of the hatred which flared into persecutions. A borrower who owed a large sum to a Jewish money-lender must have found it relatively easy to persuade himself that it was a Christian act to destroy the Jew—and the debt with him.

The ban was supposed to apply only to the obtaining of interest through money-lending. But so involved did the matter become in the hands of lawyers, both ecclesiastical and secular, that almost any transaction involving money could be called usurious, warranting punishment in this world and the next. Prudent merchants made provisions in their will for the return of all usuriously gained monies to the victims. But even the simplest and most honest

sea-going vessels   *From a contemporary woodcut*

trading required the use of money; it was necessary to give credit and reasonable to expect some compensation for the money so tied up. In order to avoid the accusation of usury, many euphemisms were employed to cover 'usurious profits'—premium, interest, consideration, gratuity, pension—words which today have a precise and respectable place in a commercial vocabulary. The charge of usury could still be invoked throughout the Renaissance and so ruin a merchant, but gradually it became a dead letter, forced to give ground to the realities of trade spread over thousands of miles and involving millions in gold.

There were fantastic profits to be made for the man who could acquire a little capital. The merchant stood behind the courageous race of seamen-explorers; when the Cape of Good Hope was at last rounded and a direct route to India established, the profits of the Arab middleman was eliminated, increasing the profits of the European merchant. It cost approximately £7,000 in modern money to provide and provision a ship for a two-year voyage which could yield some £200,000 in return. Spices from the East

37 Gathering pepper: the European buyer assesses its quality

contributed a large proportion of the profits. On 30 July 1583 there arrived in Lisbon a ship carrying 500 quintals (hundredweight) of pepper, 2,000 of cloves and cinnamon. It was not by any means an unusual cargo. The same report mentioned that there lay two more ships at the Goa station, loading 16,000 quintals of pepper, 6,000 of cloves and 1,000 of assorted spices. So regular was the spice trade that captains of the ships running it could estimate their times of arrival and departure, over half a world of water, with remarkable precision. Ships usually left either Goa or Lisbon during the last fortnight in January and arrived about mid-June.

A Fugger agent gives a vivid account of the delights and hazards of the spice trade. He wrote from Cochin-China on 10 January 1580, after a sea voyage which had lasted six months and six days, 'and during that time we saw no land, only the sea and the sky'. Five ships had left Lisbon in company but parted, each captain thinking he knew the best and quickest way to their goal. The writer's own ship encountered great storms, becalmings, and a fight with a giant shark, but in spite of the rigours of the voyage 'only 25 died on the way from Portugal to India'. Even when they landed danger was not passed: many men, accustomed to the sparseness of shipboard life, died of the high living into which they threw themselves. The main treasure to be reaped was pepper, for Cochin was the trading station to which the precious crop was brought from inland(37). The agent had established two stations, one in Goa, the other in Cochin and though he much preferred to be in Goa, where the presence of the Portuguese viceroy made for a civilised life, yet it was a wearisome journey there and back every year, 'for I must needs be present in this our pepper station'. It took six weeks to gather in the harvest and, after the departure of the ships for Portugal, there was little for him to do. 'The pepper business is profitable indeed; if none of the ships take damage in coming or going then the merchants wax rich.' Ships going out to the East carried cargoes of wine, cheese, fish, and paper, but the writer warned his master that there was little market for German goods: 'Writing tables split in the great heat; clockwork, or anything else made of iron, deteriorates at sea.' He echoes the merchant's complaint of all times—the Government was ruining the country. 'The Viceroy has increased taxes, the demand for European goods has diminished and there is as much money to be gained in organising local trade as to commit one's wares to the caprices of the sea.' All in all, 'it takes as much trouble to earn money here as in other places'. Nevertheless, he is committed to stay in Cochin for at least another five years and intends to return home by land. The journey is only 2,000 miles long and will take six months via Arabia, Persia and Turkey. 'It appears to be quite a common thing to do. I shall, however, inform myself well beforehand since I have the time to do so.'

The discovery of new overseas trade routes altered the pattern of European trade, for the developing centres now were along the Atlantic coast, the cities of London, Lisbon, Cadiz, Bristol, Antwerp, importing goods from East and West and distributing them through Europe. The ancient Italian centres fought back stubbornly. Venice(36) continued to be the 'finishing school' of traders; even the autocratic Hansa merchants were obliged to step softly in this maritime city. Elsewhere, they could behave like an occupying power; in Venice they were merely merchants. They and other German merchants were housed in the Fondaco de' Tedeschi, a handsome, three-storeyed building upon the Grand Canal(38).

Three Venetian officials took up residence there, keeping a careful watch over Venetian interests and, when the Germans left at the end of each season, they handed over the keys to the officials until their return. But even wealthy Venice began to feel the loss of that trade which ran so strongly in the north, and the other maritime cities, Genoa and Pisa particularly, gradually lost their hold.

New industries were springing up throughout Europe as a result of the inventions and discoveries of the period. Book-publishing developed into a major industry within decades of its birth; firearms and cannon of every description demanded heavy manufacturing processes, with consequent heavy investment of capital. Shipbuilding employed thousands where before there had been hundreds (*36*); between 1497 and 1612, Portugal alone sent 806 ships down the long, lonely sea-road to India; from Spain, England, and the Netherlands hundreds more were required to explore, carry cargoes, fight. It is about this time that the modern factory-owner appears on the scene, such a one as that John Winchcombe in England, a clothing manufacturer who operated 200 looms under

38   The Fondaco de' Tedeschi, Venice

one roof and was even wealthy enough to entertain Henry VIII. But he was still a rarity; most manufacture was carried out by a master craftsman and a few men working in tiny rooms. The typical member of the growing 'middle class' was the entrepreneur, the man who financed the development of new inventions, who bought low and sold high and created monopolies. The chronicler of Augsburg described such a man: 'He had the reputation of being a good Christian yet he often oppressed the common man. He would buy up at good bargains all the ash-wood, corn and wine and keep them in storage till a great demand arose for them when he would sell at very high price. No merchant worth less than 10,000 florins could compete with him.'

39 A merchant in his warehouse

In 1522 the Imperial Diet of Nuremberg studied the problem of monopolies, so grave was its effects upon the general living standards. Particular attention was drawn to the activities of merchants trading in pepper. The entire trade was in the hands of the King of Portugal, and certain companies offered to buy pepper from him at above the prevailing prices, provided that he charged their rivals an even higher price. 'Thus, and by overcharging one another, it has come to pass that spices which could originally be bought for 18 ducates the quintal are now sold at 34 ducates. Far from losing on these transactions the merchants make enormous profits; they can sell at the highest prices because nobody else in the Empire has access to the goods.' A committee of the Diet circulated the cities of Germany, asking their opinion on the subject. Augsburg returned the answer to be expected from a city grown rich on such methods. Trade was the life-blood of nations; 'big and wealthy merchants, by attracting artisans and masters, stimulate business in general. Rich companies help many small merchants by advancing them credit and loans and enabling them to become rich. How then can one say that the rich trample down the poor when they actually save them from their own incompetence and misfortunes?' The Diet, to its credit, did attempt to control the size of companies and forbade, too, any merchant from buying more than a given quantity of any one commodity in a fixed period. But the attempt was unsuccessful; the rich grew richer and the poor grew poorer as prices continued to rise.

Augsburg was the home of the greatest financial company of the period, the Fugger family. At the height of their power, the Fuggers could and did treat with monarchs as with equals: it was through their wealth that the Imperial crown was gained by Charles V. But throughout the family held firmly to the idea that they were 'in trade', not hesitating to dun even the Emperor as though he were a common debtor. The fortunes of the family were founded, humbly enough, in the 1360s by one Hans Fugger, a weaver. His goods were excellent, he was careful with his money and, when he died, he left the sum of 3,000 florins. The business remained closely linked with the family, the grandsons of Hans establishing the principle whereby all male descendants invested their money only in the family business which, in turn, provided dowries for all daughters. The first contact with the Hapsburgs was made in 1473 when the Emperor Frederic III desired to clothe his enormous entourage in cloth of the same colour. Ulrich Fugger supplied the cloth and began the association which was to bring nobility to the family but also cost it millions in gold. The basis of the Fugger fortune was the weaving and selling of cloth and later they were engaged in the lucrative spice trade. But, as other merchants had found before them, they discovered that money was to be made with money and they invested in scores of projects. Yet they found time, and money, for the creation of a charitable organisation which was more in keeping with the social reforms of the nineteenth century. The Fuggers were weavers, first and foremost, and employed a great number of men not only from Augsburg but from Italy, for the Italians were skilled in delicate work. These immigrants found themselves working for good masters who not merely demanded hard work, but gave in return something of that social security which was grossly lacking throughout the working classes in Europe. In 1520, Jacob Fugger (40) founded the Fuggerei, an estate consisting of some fifty-three houses, each of two residences, arranged in six streets. The rent for each was a mere florin a year, perhaps equivalent to one pound in today's currency, and the homes were available for their retired workmen. Even this small rent was devoted to keeping the houses in such good repair that they lasted into the twentieth century.

But if the Fuggerei was a monument to the charity of the family, the 'Golden Counting House' was the solid evidence of their wealth, a temple of finance to which devotees came from all over Europe. It was a richly panelled room whose intricate wooden carving was

40   Jacob Fugger
Drawing by Hans Burgmair

overlaid with gold-leaf. Broad windows of painted glass allowed sunlight to fall richly upon the massive armchairs, upholstered in red velvet, which stood around the walls. A great safe in one corner held some of the secrets, and a little of the wealth, of the family. Dominating the room was the master's desk, a massive structure, supported by four lions in black wood, inlaid with gold and mother-of-pearl and with a top of rare marble. Beneath the desk, a lion skin lay upon the dark, polished floor and behind it stood a great chair, its back embossed with that Fugger crest, granted by the Emperor, which had cost a king's ransom in unpaid debts. It was to this room that merchants and diplomats came to sue for financial aid, to plan great new voyages, to plot, perhaps, the downfall of some man who thought himself great. On each side of the Golden Counting House were two other houses, inhabited by the brothers who controlled the business, the whole complex forming an international clearing house for news as well as finance. Agents made their reports from all over the world, from Mexico and India, Persia and Russia, Arabia, England, China, Italy, from every country where the Fuggers had, or some day might have, their interests. The contents of the

41 The Shipping House, Lübeck, built in 1535: headquarters of the Hanseatic League

reports covered every possible subject; the assassination of a king or report of a peasant wedding, accounts of marvels, the price of pepper, or just plain gossip about mutual acquaintances. In 1570 a scholarly head of the House began to collect these reports in an ordered form. They were transmitted to history as the *Fugger News-Letters* and, in their patchy but vivid manner, give a picture of the sixteenth century rather similar to that which a newspaper file might give of the twentieth.

The Renaissance merchant was a bold, imaginative man who, though he might frequently combine with his fellows for a large undertaking, preferred to work as an individual. But, side by side with this new man, there still existed the giant Hanseatic League, born in the Middle Ages, weakening now but still formidable, presenting a stiff challenge in scores of cities. The Hansa was born of a commercial alliance between Lübeck (*41*) and Hamburg in the thirteenth century and eventually grew to wield power throughout Europe, in the sole name of profit, of a kind hitherto associated only with warrior-kings. It achieved its full growth shortly after the mid-fourteenth century when some seventy cities formed the League. Control was kept upon member cities simply by the power of boycott. The city of Bremen broke a rule against trading with Flanders, was expelled from the League and 'for the thirty miserable years which followed she was impoverished, grass grew in the streets, and poverty and desolation were everywhere within her borders'. Brunswick was later similarly punished and achieved reinstatement only when ten of her chief citizens walked barefoot through the city of Lübeck and craved pardon of the Council on their knees. There was nevertheless no lack of recruits for the Hansa operated monopolies, which made competition from non-

42   Georg Gisze, a Hanseatic merchant in London
From the portrait by Hans Holbein, 1532

44 'The Cook'
*From the painting by Pieter
Aertsen, 1559*

DOMESTIC LIFE

43   The bath tub
*Detail from 'St Elizabeth tending
Plague Victims', ascribed to Salzach,
late fifteenth century*

members almost impossible. It was essentially an inward-looking, European alliance, precisely reflecting the old trade-system of Europe. It totally ignored the new routes and the type of trade flourishing after the voyages of discovery, leaving them to be developed by the new class of merchant.

There were Hansa maintained depots, or 'factories', in some 130 European cities, the main establishments outside Germany being Nijni Novgorod in Russia, Bruges in Belgium, Bergen in Norway, and London in Britain. In the weaker cities, Hansa agents behaved with a brutal arrogance. The company of 3,000 strong established in Bergen ruled the city precisely as it wished. It had first choice of all goods brought into the city, it declined to pay taxes, used the harbours and streets as it chose and ultimately actually forced the citizens to withdraw and build a new town on the outskirts of the old. Even in the powerful and wealthy city of Novgorod, the Hansa was able to exact extraordinary conditions, not least being the provision that, in all cases of bankruptcy, Hansa merchants would be the first to be paid. They were more closely controlled in England (42) but their London 'factory' on the Thames was a favourite target for rioting mobs, so cordially were these 'Easterlings' hated by citizen and merchant alike. The employees of the Hansa, though they might strut like conquerors, were themselves prisoners of commerce. In most cities they were sworn to celibacy, living a monastic life behind the high walls of the factory. They were forbidden to have any social contact with the natives of the country in which they found themselves; day and night they were under surveillance by their superiors. Apprentices were always drawn from the parent cities in Germany. In spite of the harsh life, opportunities for private profit were great and there was no lack of newcomers. The numbers of would-be apprentices were so great, in fact, that a particularly harsh series of initiation rites were instituted to keep out the weaklings. For over 200 years the Hansa dominated in whatever trade it chose, ignoring religious or political controversy unless it interfered with profit. Its decline set in towards the end of the sixteenth century; there was no one cause, except that law which decrees that all living things must die. The fall in the demand for fish after the Reformation probably contributed; certainly Hansa merchants ignored the new trade in the West at their cost. In 1608 an English merchant gleefully recorded that 'most of their teeth have fallen out and the rest do sit but loosely in their heads'. There were others impatiently waiting to take the place of the dying giant.

HOME LIFE

The houses which today give the medieval flavour to the ancient cities of Europe will almost always be the houses of merchants, solid constructions designed to exhibit the wealth and stability of their owners and so outlasting them. The poor man's hovel disappears, the rich man's palace becomes a museum or a municipal office; but the merchant's home frequently continues as a home. He was proud of it, this visible sign of success; the painters who depicted him, robed and opulent, showed the details of his domestic background with as much care as they showed details of his face. It is no accident that the most vivid of these 'domestic interiors' should show the homes of northern merchants. Even the Italians, accustomed to the prodigal splendour of their princely courts, conceded that these merchants lived like princes, grown fat on the profits brought to their ports along the Atlantic and Baltic coasts. And, just as the prince sought fame and a brief slice of immortality by patronising the artist, so too did the merchant even if, by the irony of history, his name might be forgotten while the details of his home survive.

The house was usually on two floors, although in large cities or where space was at a premium, it might increase to three or even more. The main

45 Downstairs sitting-room, with four-poster bed door was a

46   Part of the main room of a middle-class family
From a woodcut by Albrecht Dürer, 1503

massive structure, ironbound, its massive lock and bolts supplemented with chains. It appeared, and needed to be, capable of withstanding assault; each man guarded his own, and riot was a commonplace. The door opened immediately into a main room and, inside, it was seen that the house was essentially a shell subdivided by wooden partitions. There was no opportunity for, and therefore little sense of the need for, privacy; rooms connected immediately with each other for the space-wasting corridor could be employed only in large buildings. It was quite common for the bedroom to serve also as sitting-room, members of the household or even guests moving casually around whether or no the occupant was in bed. In wealthy homes, this last was a massive structure, almost a small room in itself. The four-poster bed, which came into general use in the sixteenth century, was a considerable advance upon the towering, unprotected beds of earlier years (45). Curtains were hung around it, not only protecting its occupants from the cold draughts of an unheated room but also giving a measure of privacy. Beneath it

47 A dining-room *Woodcut by Hans Sachs*

48   Kitchen with an enclosed stove

there was usually a smaller bed to be pulled out at night for a
servant or child.

Downstairs the same doubling of function was apparent in the
other rooms; the separate dining-room came in much later, and
then only for the very wealthy, and the whole operation of prepar-
ing and serving a meal took place in one room (64). The simplicity
of eating habits continued well into the sixteenth century. There
were only two meals in the day: dinner at 10 a.m. and supper at
5 p.m. Dining utensils were limited, the same plate, knife and
spoon being used for every course. Glass was rare, mugs or goblets
of metal being used. In the middle of the sixteenth century choco-
late appeared as a drink and, later, coffee and tea, but it was very
long before these found their way into the lower ranks of society.
Ale and light wine was the universal drink for both sexes, and
all ages and classes; a gallon a day was considered a reasonable
quantity and it was drunk less from choice than from necessity.
Pure water was almost as difficult to find in cities as it was on ships.

The open fire was the main source of both heating and cooking.
The fireplace was large enough for a man to stand in, and the
burning logs were supported on iron implements whose design
was to change little over the next two centuries. The advent of the
chimney in the late thirteenth century was probably one of the

biggest domestic advances in Europe, enabling even the poorer families to cook at home instead of at the common bakehouse. The contribution the Renaissance made was the enclosed stove (*48*); this developed in Germany and then spread throughout the Continent, bringing with it the means to conserve heat, thereby using it far more economically. Interiors of houses were, of necessity, rather dark. Glass for windows had been introduced as early as the thirteenth century, but even by the sixteenth glass-makers had not progressed beyond the stage of making small, opaque sections. In order to use them in the large area required, it was necessary to set them in strips of lead, a device which made an attractive pattern but further reduced the available light. But, even with this limitation, the north showed a considerable advantage over the south. In Italy, the long months of fine weather made unnecessary the provision of expensive glass for windows. Window apertures were provided only with shutters, often richly covered

with fabric. In winter, very little light could have entered the house, for there was no choice between enduring the winter cold and closing the shutters. Rushes still provided the most common form of floor-covering in the north, as they had done for centuries. They were cheap, absorbed moisture and acted as crude insulation—and a fruitful breeding ground for vermin. In spite of the prevailing indifference to hygiene, most houses would boast a bath—literally a tub(*43*), usually placed in the bedroom and often shared by two people at a time in order to save hot water. The only available source of heating in most cities was wood. The medieval habit of communal bathing in public

49 Living room of a wealthy family
Detail from Van Eyck's 'St Barbara'

baths had disappeared, largely through the fear of the spreading of diseases. The householder therefore had to provide his own bath, and wood for heating, in most large cities, was very expensive.

50 Carved *cassone* from Florence, fifteenth century

The furnishings of the house would appear sparse by modern standards, but it was in the provision of specialised, elaborate pieces of furniture that these homes showed the greatest difference from those of earlier periods. In place of the simply-made trestle table and bench, there appeared the heavy, elaborately carved table and separate chairs, the latter often upholstered in leather. The plain chest became a major article of furniture. In the absence of large cupboards, some form of freestanding container for clothes, linen and even crockery was necessary and, bulking large in the room as it did, it was natural that considerable care should be taken with its appearance. In Germany and England particularly these great wooden chests were richly carved; in Italy they were painted. Some of the most distinctive work of the Renaissance was lavished upon the *cassone*, the chest which a bride took with her as part of her dowry (50).

The elaborate decoration of essentials, together with the proud display of inessentials, was an indication of the new wealth flowing through society. There was enough money left over, after the necessities of life had been provided, to indulge in that conspicuous consumption which is a hallmark of a mercantile society. The medieval householder had been, perforce, content with perhaps a shrine as the only ornament in the house; his successor could scatter a variety of attractive, expensive and useless objects about his rooms (49). The tapestries which clothed the walls were of great practical use as well as of considerable expense, but the jugs and vases of precious metals, the mirror or two, together with a medallion or plaque, the heavy, bound books upon a carved table—these were intended to proclaim to the world the owner's success in diverting into his own pockets some of the gold of Europe.

Chapter IV

THE COMMON MAN

THE closing years of the Middle Ages and the opening years of the Renaissance were marked by violent, if hopeless, rebellions of the lower classes, eruptions from that sullen pool which was masked by the glittering surface of the new society. The old order was disintegrating under new pressures throughout Europe. That same spirit, which discovered the lands of the New World, challenged the authority of the Papacy, revealed the past, reached out into the Universe to drag the stars closer, was at work lower down the social scale. But there it was transmuted into bitterness and rebellion. Little enough of the flood of gold found its way downwards. The rich merchant could eat heartily of the new delicacies—strawberries, apricots, currants; the poor man paid twice as much for the wheat which was still his main food. The spiritual and political dominance of the Papacy might have been destroyed, but destroyed too were innumerable charities which had eased the lot of poor men in a society which saw no especial reason to legislate for the weak. Envy was brought closer home as the ancient social hierarchy of society crumbled: once, the poor man could merely admire from afar the activities of his spiritual and temporal lords; now, overnight his neighbour might become a wealthy man. The world seemed full of men strutting in silks and satins, gained at the expense of the poor.

It is a simple enough task to identify the great and powerful for their records are to be found everywhere. They have their biographers, their portrait painters; their magnificent costumes exist still or can be discerned in their portraits; their palaces endure; their names remain. But the common man is merely a part of the background against which these glittering figures move. He is a member of a defeated or victorious army, one of a ravening mob, one of the thousands of plague victims, who will be mentioned in conjunction with the victory or the death of a great man. Only a handful of writers attempted to bring him out of the background;

THE COMMON MAN

Chaucer in England, Sachetti in Italy were among those few who discerned his importance and accorded to a swineherd, a seaman, a pedlar, the literary immortality usually reserved for a prince. These apart, the common man is usually visible only through the eyes of his superiors, appearing as an item in the records of the king's taxes or an employer's payroll; recorded by civic authorities who attempt to regulate his costume, punish his crimes and, occasionally, feed or clothe him. He is inarticulate and virtually defenceless save in brief spasms of corporate rage, when he and his fellows in their thousands will almost destroy their own city. His few poor possessions vanish with him; the cheap clothes resembling sacking soon rot, his home collapses or is razed and no one troubles to record the disappearance of a one-room cabin in a filthy slum. To find the common man therefore it is necessary to trace him through the organisation of society around him.

THE URBAN WORKER

The lowest social system in which it is possible to find a coherent pattern is the guild. It was a system, slowly being eroded by the new industrialism, which had emphasised the singleness of society. Every master had once been an apprentice; every apprentice could hope to be a master. Each guild was exclusive, one existing for members of every distinct trade—furriers, tanners, bakers, goldsmiths—protecting them from interference from outside and disciplining them within the guild. The system was so powerful that any member who broke a labour law was haled before the mayor in the Guildhall rather than before the court of the monarch. The guilds had fought long and bitterly for their rights. They held no nonsensical ideas of free trade but created monopolies by their very existence, jealously reserving for their members the rights of manufacture and sale of specific goods. The intake of apprentices was carefully controlled for, if the members of any one guild became greater than a locality could support, then the profits of all were reduced. The son of a freeman could always count on being accepted, sometimes without premium; children of non-freemen always had to pay a premium and were admitted only when a vacancy occurred.

The limitation of the number of apprentices was not only designed to produce a steady, if limited, flow of masters, but to ensure that a master did not take on more apprentices than he could effectively control. The guilds were very much aware that the price they paid for a monopoly was that the standards of their goods must be first-class. Apprenticeship was therefore a means of training a man thoroughly in the mysteries of his craft (51). It was a lengthy and arduous period for a high-spirited youth. His indentures were irrevocable on both sides and he received no payment during the period—anything up to twelve years—while he was under his master. The master, on his side, took the youth into his household, kept him in necessities, chastised him when required, and paid him a set sum at the end of his term. His apprenticeship concluded, the youth became a journeyman, free to work for whom he pleased within his craft. Technically, the journeyman was hired by the day, from which practice came his name. In certain classes of work which required a continuity of process, such as weaving (58), he was usually hired for as long as the work lasted whether it were for a week or a year. It was usual for journeymen in search of employment to assemble in some public place at a particular time. Such a practice, although it seems to hint more of the slave-market than the hiring of free men, was a protection for the workers. An engagement entered between master and man under the sharp eyes of other craftsmen ensured that no man would accept wages beneath the minimum. The masters also approved of the practice, for it prevented any one of them employing cheap labour and thereby being able to undersell his rivals. The working day was, quite literally, a day—from 5 a.m. to 8 p.m. between March and September and from dawn till dusk in winter. The men usually had half an hour for breakfast at about 9 a.m., and an hour and a half for dinner in the afternoon.

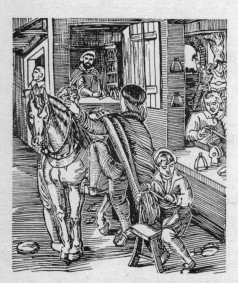

51 An apprentice stirrup-maker at work

52   'The Card Players'
From the painting by Lucas van Leyden, c. 1514

53   'The Harvesters'
Detail from the painting by Pieter Bruegel, 1565

54 Washing Day
From a German illumination of 1582
(British Museum Harleian MS. 3469, f. 32v.)

The journeyman could, and often did, remain a simple day-labourer for the rest of his life. But it was also open to him to enter the ranks of masters by means of an examination and the presentation of his 'masterpiece', some object of his craft made to satisfy the rigorous examination (55). The use of the word today has been limited to works of high art, but the term also covered, for example, the correct tanning of a skin by tanners, the correct dismembering of a carcass by butchers. The journeyman, having satisfied his examiners, could in his turn set up shop and employ apprentices and journeymen.

55 Journeyman mason and carpenter undergoing a guild examination before a warden of the guild

He would probably continue to work side by side with his men; there were great and wealthy masters but the majority were simply 'master-craftsmen', small, independent men employing two or three others, and producing most that was required for a civilisation.

The system began to crumble during the sixteenth century, weakened from within by the short-sighted selfishness of the master-craftsmen. The admittance of journeymen into their number was at their discretion. It was therefore a simple matter to ensure that a favoured journeyman—a son, a nephew, a relative of a friend—received a perfunctory examination, while the examination for others became more and more exacting. The numbers of men forced to remain journeymen increased, foreshadowing the 'working class' of the nineteenth and twentieth centuries. The French government, which more than any other attempted to control the details of working life, made some effort to stop the process. It was ordained that no more than three months should be taken for the making of a masterpiece and that a journeyman could appeal to a jury appointed by a judge. But, as processes became more complex, and industries larger, it became increasingly difficult for an ordinary man to find the capital to set himself up in business. The guilds themselves were becoming less independent, so that master-drapers became virtual employees of the weavers and master-printers fell into dependence upon the booksellers. The smaller guilds fought back stubbornly, resisting to the end that distribution of labour which is the foundation of modern industry. Some recognised the necessity of combining with a related trade and allowed their members to be simultaneously members of that trade. But the making of the masterpiece remained the final test and the would-be master was obliged to perform all stages of the work. 'The future hatter was given a pound of wool and other raw materials, and had to produce a finished hat, dyed and trimmed with velvet. He had to do everything himself, from fulling the wool to placing the feathers in position.'

It became increasingly obvious that such a method of working was wasteful in both time and materials, the end product being therefore far more expensive than it need. The great woollen industry had long recognised the fact, establishing a precedent for others to follow. Wool was the universal clothing material; all classes in all countries were dependent upon it for their wardrobe in greater or lesser degree. It provided constant employment for thousands, from the shepherd who tended the sheep to the tailor who made the finished product. But the nature of the material is such that it was impossible for any one man to control personally all the processes from beginning to end. The tailor was

56   The first stage of the wool
industry: shearing

dependent upon the weaver, the weaver upon the spinner (57), the spinner upon the shearer (56), and at each stage there were other subsidiary processes, of which dyeing was the most important. One of the greatest cloth centres in the late Middle Ages was in Florence and there the industry was divided into two great guilds, the Arte della Lana and the Calimala, the former making the cloth and the latter finishing it for the market. Eventually, the Arte della Lana developed into wool brokers, scouring the continent for supplies and employing hundreds in the production of the raw cloth, most of them working in their own homes. The most vital part of the Calimala's task was the dyeing of the cloth, an expensive and delicate operation which the Florentines brought to a high peak of skill. The demand for their product did not fail until towards the end of the fifteenth century, when the great English woollen industry began to get into its stride, and it was upon the Calimala that the great Florentine fortunes were founded.

57 The next stage of the wool industry: spinning. This was conducted on a casual basis as a cottage industry

The three basic elements of the industry—weaving (58), fulling, and dyeing, were firmly organised into craft guilds, but the simple preliminary preparations of the raw wool, such as carding and spinning, were tasks that could be conducted on a casual basis. It would, indeed, have been difficult to prevent it being so conducted. The raw wool, after being sheared, would naturally pass through the hands of the peasant's wife. Originally, she would have prepared the wool for her own use, but, as supplies increased to match the growth of the demand, so the preparation of wool became a cottage industry in its own right. It suited the peasant, for it brought in a little more money and it also suited the wealthy controllers of the industry. Their overheads were lower and, in the

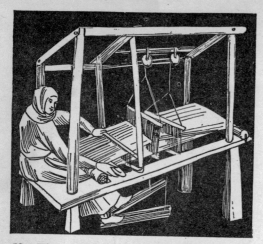

58 The wool industry: weaving. This stage of manufacture formed one of the three major guilds of the industry

absence of an organised labour force, they could make their own wage rates. It emphatically did not suit the town workers, who saw their carefully erected structure of price and wage agreements being undermined, as well as employment being taken from them. Their objection frequently took the form of physical violence, gangs of workers from the towns raiding the surrounding villages, breaking the dyeing vats of cottagers, destroying the cloth and attempting to terrorise their rivals. But the peasant needed the money, the tailor needed the cloth, and the once proud weaving guilds were forced to bow to the inevitable. A few maintained independence but grew at the expense of their colleagues; the majority of workers degenerated into day-labourers, their numbers reducing their bargaining power so that they were forced to accept whatever the few great masters chose to pay.

The guild system had many defects. The more wealthy guilds dominated the poorer, even attempting to exclude them from municipal offices. In the Italian cities, friction between the guilds was constant, ranging from simple rivalry to bloody warfare as the lesser strove to obtain a larger share of the city's prosperity and the greater strove to maintain the *status quo*. Guilds flourished generally in the wealthier cities, the poor cities and all rural areas being ignored. They exercised, as a matter of course, a degree of control over their members which the most tyrannical trade union today would hesitate to employ for emergencies. Yet, with all their defects, they encouraged a social cohesion and when they disappeared a gulf opened in society between the few and the many, between the employer and the employed. There appeared a new class in Europe, the landless, workless vagabond (59), the 'sturdy beggar' who, under other circumstances, would have been a sturdy workman. The class appeared in force in the north, particularly in England and was recruited from a number of sources. The suppression of the monasteries not only destroyed the refuge of the truly poor, as well as of the idlers, but also took away the source of livelihood of innumerable men. The great institutions were larger than many of their attendant villages and their day-to-day running absorbed the energies of a substantial proportion of the labour market. But the largest number of vagabonds were the victims of the new, large-scale operation of production which, in rural areas, found expression in the enclosure of common lands. The counterpart of the degraded city craftsman was the dispossessed peasant forced to be a day-labourer—if labour could be found. Ignoring, or mistaking, the cause, authority treated the sturdy beggar almost as though he were a criminal. Some provision had to be made for him, but the principle adopted was to make relief so odious that a man would prefer to wander and starve, or turn into a genuine criminal.

The intellectual spirit of the Renaissance was itself a tragic cause of the degradation of the ordinary workman. Education hitherto, though narrow in breadth, had been freely available to all classes; there was, at least, an equality of ignorance. The new methods of education required specialisation: Greek and Latin was its basis and an intimate knowledge of a long-dead world its object. No working man could hope to touch even the fringes of this beautiful new world of the mind.

59 Vagabonds
From Barclay's 'Ship of Fools', 1509

'Only men of noble birth can obtain perfection. The poor, who work with their hands and have no time to cultivate their minds, are incapable of it.' So said Lorenzo de' Medici, the great patron of the arts. The statement was brutally true and expressed the attitude of the higher to the lower classes. There was a compensation; an exceptionally gifted man, whether artist or merchant, could now move upwards in society, but once he had crossed the gulf he disassociated himself totally from his origins, thus maintaining the division. The artist became distinct from, and superior to, the craftsman, whereas before they had been one. The origins of the painters, sculptors, and architects who emblazoned Europe lay in the same humble workroom where the apprentice house-painter or mason learnt his trade. But as the one was adopted by princes, the other went a little deeper into obscurity, his skill becoming a little narrower, his life becoming that much less rich. A part of the price Europe paid for the monuments of the Renaissance was the squalor of the industrial cities of the nineteenth century. The artist needed still to be a craftsman but there was no necessity for the craftsman to be an artist, and it was he who, eventually, built the industrial cities and made their artefacts.

THE RURAL WORKER

Serfdom had almost disappeared throughout Europe. It had survived, by over two centuries, the feudal system which created it; indeed, in Scotland, it was not finally abolished until 1799, when the serfs in the salt and coalmines were declared free, and in England as late as 1561 the Duke of Norfolk was able to claim a man as his bondman. But as a practical system it was dead and, theoretically, slavery had at last departed from the Continent and all men were free. In practice, the successor of the serf was probably far worse off. The serf had been a slave only in relationship to his lord; with regard to other men he had most of the rights of a free man—with some privileges of his own. He could even become a knight—a fact recognised by the law, which specified that he would automatically become free if he attained knighthood. He could not be held to a contract, and many a free man found himself holding a piece of useless paper when the party with whom he had contracted in all good faith repudiated it, claiming serfdom. In return for his services, his lord had certain minimum obligations towards him. There was no particular rejoicing among the Scottish serfs when they received their freedom; they declared instead that it was merely a trick whereby their lord could escape the traditional payment to the wife of a serf who bore a child.

No man held himself responsible for the well-being of the peasant and neither did he have even the weakening protection of the guild. The land which he tilled could never belong to him; its ownership was divided and subdivided, tenant was superimposed upon tenant, but the law ensured that, no matter what the landlord's extravagances, his ultimate claim was always sound. The new merchants bought lands as one of the few ways open to them for social ostentation which the sumptuary laws did not forbid. They proved themselves no more competent than the previous noble owners who wasted their substance at court. The land deteriorated; but it was the tiller of the land who paid taxes, not the landlord; it was he, his neighbours and his sons, who provided the backbone of the army. In the later Middle Ages the tendency had been for the cultivator to be tacitly recognised as the owner but as land grew more expensive the owners rights were revived. The yeomanry in England were protected by a sensible government as 'the backbone of the army and the principal surety of taxation', and by the mid-sixteenth century there were probably

60   Village life: preparations for the winter

as many small proprietors in England as there were tenant-farmers. These latter were less fortunate; the vast fortunes to be made from wool were an incentive to the landlord to dispossess his tenants and turn his land over to sheep. Elizabeth I forbade any landowner to possess more than 2,000 sheep, and though Government edicts were, as ever, evaded as often as they were obeyed yet they exercised some control in favour of the small people. The English farm-worker enjoyed relative comfort and security. He could not leave his employment before a year was past, and even then only with a certificate from his master and at harvest time he could be compelled to return. But neither could his master dismiss him without notice and his wages were fixed by the local justice of the peace. Meat found its way into his diet, as well as the ubiquitous salt fish, and his drink was both strong and varied.

The serf in France was changed into the *metayer*. He was a man without capital, paying his rent in kind, usually half the harvest. He was dependent upon his proprietor for seeds and tools and, in a bad year, for all other necessities of life. It was a system which could have suited neither party. In a bad year the landlord received nothing but had to support a starving man and his family; in a good year he received a glut of produce. The *metayer* himself would rarely have the chance to accumulate cash to make himself independent. When, or if, he did he could become a *fermier*, striking a balance one year with the next and paying his rent in cash. It was to his own interest that he should cultivate the land properly, for all profits went into his own pockets.

In the early sixteenth century treatises on husbandry began to appear but it was long before their theory became even limited practice. European farming was primitive, lagging behind other parts of the world. A classic example of its limitations was shown in Spain when the lands of the Moors were turned over to Spanish farmers. That same land which, through generations of patient care, was able to support a thriving population, reverted back to its natural aridity within a generation in Spanish hands. Elsewhere in Europe the hallowed system of common lands was responsible for the general deterioration. 'Common ownership is one long devastation and brigandage' a Frenchman asserted during the bitter controversy over enclosures. The enclosing of land did indeed rob the peasant of free grazing but he was robbed of very little; that which was everyone's property was no one's responsibility.

61 Outside a country inn
Detail from 'The Peasant Dance' by Pieter Bruegel, c. 1568

62   The lord and his bailiff

From an early sixteenth-century illumination in a French translation of an agricultural treatise by Piero de Crescenzi

(British Museum Add. MS. 19720, f. 63v.)

Common lands were opened between June and March; each man naturally wanted his cattle to be the first to graze, with the result that the pasture never had time to recover and the grass provided thin, rank fodder. Cattle weighed perhaps a third of their present-day weight; sheep frequently yielded less than one pound of wool per animal. There was little manure for cultivated lands, for cattle wandered at will and the only

63   An English shepherd
From Spenser's 'Shepherd's Calendar', 1579

assistance given the soil was to allow it to rest two years in three—a wasteful system which did little to restore life to the soil. Lack of variety in crops was a fundamental reason for the poorness of the land, and the discovery that certain plants, such as the bean, actually enriched it was an advance in agriculture comparable to that made at sea by the discovery of the compass. Yet the few who attempted the new methods of crop rotation found themselves hampered by tradition. Between the two dates fixed for harvest and ploughing (*62*), the proprietor ceased to be the owner of his land, the flocks of the village roaming over it as of right, trampling down any new crop that appeared after the traditional date.

There nevertheless began the trend towards mixed farming which was of incalculable benefit to the health of all classes. During the sixteenth century vegetables began to appear in the field and on the table, some brought from the New World, others painstakingly developed from poor native stock: cabbages, carrots, lettuces, maize, potatoes, cauliflowers (*44*)—all humble plants but of truly greater value to the people of Europe than all the shiploads of gold. In the past, the tables of even the rich had shown an incredible monotony of diet. Meat in all its forms was present: venison, beef, game birds of every kind, fish, served separately or together in a great pie and heavily spiced. The spices served as much to disguise the rancid flavour of insufficiently preserved meat as well as a preservation medium and the quantities used were such as to dull the palate to subtler flavours. Fruit was available but was expensive, while vegetables were almost totally lacking. The diet of the poor was correspondingly unbalanced. Bread was synonymous with food and when the harvests failed the most desperate measures were employed to find a substitute for wheat: acorns, barks of trees, ordinary grass seed, even earth was mixed with a few precious ounces of wheat flour to stifle the pangs of hunger. The eating of fresh meat was a luxury and the lack of green vegetables was probably responsible for those scores of obscure skin diseases which went under the general heading of leprosy. The development of cheap, nutritious green plants gave a badly needed balance to the diet of all, while the introduction of potatoes and maize from the Americas provided an insurance against the periodic famines occasioned by failure of the wheat harvest.

The potato (65) was probably first discovered by the Spaniards in Peru about 1530. The Peruvians surrounded its cultivation with a

64   Interior of an Italian farmhouse

whole ritual of magic, for the curious plant formed a vital part of their economy, valued higher than the gold which the Europeans had come to plunder. It is not an exciting dish and probably little was made of it, beyond its curiosity value, when it appeared in Spain sometime in the 1550s. Nevertheless, its value as a cheap, filling and nutritious vegetable was well established within a decade of its appearance, and it made a slow advance northward through Europe. It was brought to England in 1584 directly from North America, where Raleigh's ill-fated colony in Virginia had cultivated it as a main-stay of subsistence. For

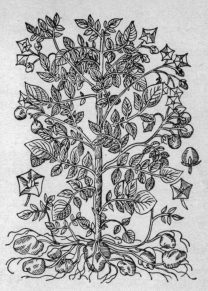

65   The Virginia potato

the common people of Europe it was a gift from God; unlike the aristocratic wheat it grew on poor soils, its cultivation did not require expensive animals and equipment and, above all, it could be grown in fields or gardens, wherever there was room for the tubers to spread. Even one plant, growing in a minute area, would provide a good meal for an entire family.

Europeans encountered maize nearly forty years before the potato, but it was slower in establishing itself as an article of diet in Europe. In 1492 Columbus noted that it formed the staple diet of the Mexicans and brought home a few ears as a curiosity. Its strange taste was probably emphasised by its superficial resemblance to the familiar wheat and it was cultivated at first only as cattle-food. But inevitably a hungry man cooked and ate it without ill effect, and it found its place on the tables of the poor. By the end of the century it had begun to oust wheat as the major foodstuff in southern Europe, spreading eventually to the south-east. It brought with it a heavy penalty, however. The easiest way to cook it was in the form of porridge; the cheapest way to eat it was by itself, for it was both filling and pleasant to the taste. Maize eaten in this form, however, did not provide all the vitamins required, so that a deficiency disease, similar to beriberi, developed among those peoples who attempted to live exclusively upon it. It was not until the eighteenth century that the disease was officially noticed and named 'pellagra', indicating the roughening of the skin which accompanied the first stage. It was then believed to be a combination of scurvy and leprosy, so bad was its appearance, and another century was to pass before its true nature was discovered.

THE MILLER AND THE BAKER

The biggest single piece of machinery with which most people came in contact was the mill (66). Legends and tales were woven around it, for not only did it mark the civilised from the primitive, distinguishing between those who must wearily grind their basic food by hand from those who enslaved the elements to the task, but the structure itself seemed a living thing. Quivering and groaning as wind or water performed their task, its dim interior thunderous with the sound of the grinding stones, producing as it did the ultimate food, there was little wonder that it entered folklore tinged with dread. The Devil was a miller, grinding the souls of men; fragments of the mill itself could cure diseases; its ceaseless clangor seemed to be the voice of the rural spirits long suppressed by Christianity.

The water-mill was a Roman invention and dominated Europe for nearly 2,000 years. But it was not until the fourteenth century that the windmill began to spread in northern Europe, developing first in the Low Countries whose slow moving streams made the water-mill less efficient. The great cost of construction and its social importance made the mill a communal investment. Later its ownership passed to the owner of the land, and the miller ceased to be an official of the community but became instead an official of the lord. It was probably this fact which made the miller the universally hated man that he was. All men had to bring their wheat to the mill for grinding, not only through necessity but by law, and the miller took a substantial fraction of the flour, as he was legally entitled. His customers were convinced that, as a matter of course, he stole, substituting fine sand for the flour he abstracted. Laws were passed to prevent his dishonesty; his customers were supposed to weigh the wheat immediately before grinding and the flour immediately after. But still, sand found its

66   Windmills: a tower mill (*left*) and a post mill (*right*)

way into the flour. Even if he were honest, the miller could plague
the life of his neighbours. He alone could control the complicated
mechanism of his mill, knew how to adjust the large, heavy stones
so that flour of any quality could be obtained; a rash, inexperienced
man could destroy the mill during a storm; a too-cautious man
would lose valuable working time for fear of the wind's power.
The man who wanted his wheat ground, therefore, had to wait
upon the pleasure of the miller. There were never lacking customers,
save in times of famine and then the miller could become a seller
of flour.

The baker (67) was as important in the city as the miller was in
the country. Few households had the necessary equipment to make
bread regularly for a large family; the dough was usually prepared
and taken to the town bakers in the evening and received back as
bread in the morning. The numbers of bakers were controlled by
the guild, an apprentice serving a term of some three years. His
'masterpiece' often took the form of a banquet given to the
masters of his guild, for his trade included the making of luxury
confections as well as plain bread. His customers tended to be as
suspicious of him as the countrymen were of the miller, for it was
difficult to relate the weight of dough handed in with the weight of
bread taken out. Inspectors examined both the quality and weight
of his bread, exacting fines or even corporal punishment for any

that fell below standard. His working life was harder than that of other master-craftsmen; he toiled when other men were asleep; able to pay the wages of only a few apprentices, for there was little money in his trade; liable, above all, to the respiratory disease peculiar to his profession, caused by the inhalation of flour dust. His was a trade which had changed little over the past 4,000 years and which, in spite of modern machinery, has changed little in its essentials today.

67   Working in the bakery

Chapter V

THE CITY

THE Age of the City had achieved its most brilliant flowering, but already there were indications that it was dying. It had been a violent, but inspiring, age, tracing its origin back 3,000 years to those city-states of Greece which had given birth to the ideal of free men ruling themselves. For, essentially, the city consisted of a group of men who, after generations of conflict among themselves, had evolved a workable system of self-government. That system varied from city to city; in any one of them the proportion of men who could claim full citizenship was always small, the great mass of people still little more than serfs, exerting their rights only through the medium of fierce rebellions against the upper classes. Yet throughout Europe, in Italy, Germany, and the Low Countries in particular there had been a common agreement as to the ends if not the means of government —a society in which most of the rulers were chosen by some of the ruled. Out of the civic concept arose endless and bloody wars; the price the citizens paid for their freedom was measured precisely by their willingness to bear arms in defence of their city against its rivals.

The true voice of the city was the great bell, of town hall or cathedral, which bellowed the alarm on the approach of armed citizens of an enemy city, summoning all able men to walls and gates. The Italians, indeed, took the bell and made of it a moving shrine, a kind of civic Ark which led the armies to battle. Battles against neighbouring cities for the possession of a scrap of farmland; battles against the Emperor or the king for civic rights; battles against hordes of wandering soldiery; during all these, the economic life of the city came to a standstill. All fit men between the ages of 15 and 70, without exception, were taken from their normal activities to fight. So, at length, for the sake of economic survival, professionals were hired to fight the wars, while at the same time civic power began to fall into the hands of a prominent citizen.

Controlling money and arms.as he did, the citizen evolved into the prince in the once free cities. In those countries which acknowledged a central monarchy, city and throne made peace through exhaustion; some cities, such as London, retained much of their autonomy; others were absorbed totally into the framework of monarchy. Nevertheless, throughout the Renaissance, cities continued still as living units, discharging for themselves most of the functions which in modern society fall to the jurisdiction of the central authority. They were not the dormitories or industrial centres or pleasure gardens that so many were to become, but seemingly organic structures of flesh and brick with their own, identifiable, rhythm of life.

THE SHAPE OF THE CITY

The cities which studded Europe like jewels were already ancient, coming down through the centuries curiously regular in shape and constant in size. Only in England was the sense of symmetry absent, for the English cities, with a few exceptions, had not been planned as such but grew up from humble beginnings and remained amorphous as building was haphazardly added to building. The continental tendency had been to found new cities rather than to expand the old to unmanageable proportions; in Germany alone, 2,400 had been founded over some 400 years. In terms of population, they would today be called towns or even large villages. Orange in France numbered only 6,000 souls until well into the nineteenth century. A city of a quarter of a million inhabitants was a giant and there were few of those. Milan, the capital of a dukedom, held 200,000, twice the size of its great rival, Florence (*68, 94*), for size was not necessarily an indication of power. Rheims, the place of coronation and a great commercial city, numbered 100,000, Paris perhaps 250,000. A figure ranging between 10,000 and 50,000 would apply to most European cities. Even the ravages created by the plague had no long-term effect upon the static nature of population. The totals of plague deaths were always exaggerated but, nevertheless, perhaps a quarter of the population would be carried off within a few months; yet, within a generation, the city would return to its original level. Overspill population found their way into the new cities. The Italian pattern, followed in greater or lesser degree throughout Europe, was that of a number of cities, linked by conquest or

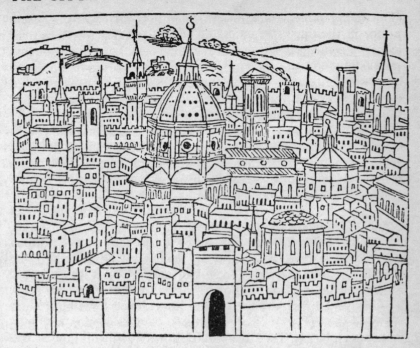

68   Florence in the late fifteenth century
From a contemporary woodcut

commercial federation, around a single giant. Systems of government and local customs peculiar to each city in the federation were
jealously preserved but taxation and defence were controlled from
the centre.

A city expanded as a tree does, retaining its shape but increasing
its size, the city walls, like tree rings, marking growth. It was the
poorer classes who lived immediately outside the walls, beggars,
outcasts, men with humble trades, who would build hovels
against the city wall, forming a vile ring of squalid streets outside
the city. Occasionally they would be the target of an energetic
municipality but usually they would be allowed to remain until
some pattern became evident. The well-to-do lived in an outer
ring of villas in large grounds, protected by their own walls. When
at length civic pride or economic necessity required an expansion
of the city, a new circuit of walls would be traced outside the old,
encompassing the new growth and leaving space for more. The old

walls would remain, possibly for centuries afterwards, or were cannibalised to make new buildings. Cities tended to renew their form, not their material, so that the same piece of brick or squared stone might have a life of a thousand years or more in half a dozen different buildings. The sites of those walls which have disappeared can still be traced, for they later provided valuable, ready-made ring-roads or, less often, public gardens.

The city walls were the factor which governed shape and size. During the Middle Ages they had been the ultimate in defence for a city well supplied with water and food. A general contemplating a siege would have to be prepared to spend months waiting for the enemy's supplies to run out. The walls were maintained at the public expense; whatever else was allowed to fall into ruin, they took priority in the allocation of funds. A collapsed wall was an indication of a collapsing city, and the first task of a victorious general was to raze the walls if he did not intend to occupy the city. The gradual decline in the importance of walls was reflected in the changing methods of portraying a city. The plan view came in extensively during the sixteenth century; it was a method which enhanced the importance of the streets, communication triumphing over insulation. The streets were shown lined with houses, the prominent buildings still appeared but gradually all was flattened, formalised as the plan became more accurate—and less visually interesting. But before the plan view, the custom had been to show the city as a traveller might view it from a distant road so that it appeared in art as it was in reality, a single unit with walls, towers, churches blending together as though it were one great castle (69). Such cities exist still and those such as Verona, that lie on a hillside, show very clearly the form which their builders gave them. In the south, particularly in Italy, a dominant feature was the great towered houses which gave to some cities the appearance of a petrified forest. These houses were relics of a more violent age, when faction and family feuds rent the cities so that those who could built ever higher and higher to achieve advantage over their neighbour. Successive city governments had managed to reduce their number, but many still towered, a threat to internal security, robbing the narrow streets of air and light.

The gates (70) which pierced the walls played a double role, for not only were they part of the defences but they contributed to the city's revenue. Officers were stationed at them to levy tax on

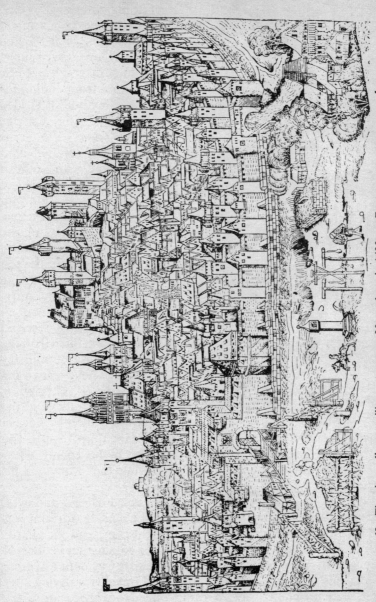

69   The city wall as a military structure: Nuremberg in 1493   *From a contemporary woodcut*

everything entering the city. Sometimes the goods might be the produce of fields and gardens of the nearby country; sometimes they were exotic spices come from thousands of miles away but all yielded up tax at the gate. On one occasion when Florentine revenues were running dangerously low, an official suggested that the number of gates should be doubled, thereby doubling the revenue. He was laughed out of the council chamber but his unthinking suggestion arose out of the prevailing idea that the city was an independent entity. The country people loathed the taxes, for they received little more from them than the dubious promise of military protection. They went to extreme lengths to avoid paying, and Sachetti's story of the farmer who concealed eggs in

70 The town gate, at which tolls on all goods passing into the city were exacted

his baggy trousers with intent to defraud has the ring of truth. The guards at the gate, who had been informed by his enemy, courteously insisted that he should be seated while they examined his baggage.

In cities controlled by a lord, the gates acted as ears and eyes. They were the only point of contact with the outside world; it was from the outside world that his main threat came and the guards at the gates kept him closely informed of the comings and goings of foreigners. In free cities, the closing of the gate was both a symbol and a means of independence. The belated traveller, arriving after sunset, had no choice but to camp outside—whence arose the custom of building inns just outside the main gates. These gates appeared as small fortresses, housing the garrison of the city and, indeed, the great castles which dominated the medieval cities were usually merely extensions of the main gate-houses.

The lack of plan in late medieval cities was more apparent than real. True, the streets seem to wander without object, to curl and coil back upon themselves or even peter out in a backyard, but they were intended less to provide access from one point to another of the city than to provide a setting for communal life. A stranger passing through a gate would find his way without difficulty to the heart of the city, for the main roads radiated from the central square. *Piazza, place, platz*—whatever it might be called in the native language—it was the descendant of the Roman *forum*, the place where men rallied in times of war or lingered in times of peace. Again, only in England was this meeting place absent, the English usually preferring to widen their high street for the market; it served the same purpose but lacked the sense of unity and, when traffic increased, lost its value as a central meeting-place. But on the Continent this echo of Rome continued. It could be humble—an unpaved area shaded by trees, perhaps, and lined with a ragged row of buildings. It could be stupendous, as the great square of Siena or Venice (71), planned as a unit so that it seems like a vast, roofless hall. But whatever its appearance, it was the city made visible, the place of congregation, and flanking it would be the vital organs of the city, the centres of government and justice. Elsewhere in the city

71 Piazza San Marco, Venice

there would be another great natural centre: the cathedral with its ancillary buildings, frequently set in a smaller square. From city-gate to square, to cathedral, the road would run wide enough and clean enough and straight enough. But away from the centres the streets would be local veins serving local needs. They were made deliberately narrow, as much to provide shelter from sun or rain as to conserve space, and sometimes the upper storeys of houses would be a bare few feet apart. The narrowness of the streets acted as a military defence for the citizens; the first act of an occupying power would be to gallop through them before barricades could be erected. It was virtually impossible for a military force to keep any semblance of order while marching through them and, under these conditions, a hostile crowd armed only with cobblestones could keep a professional force at bay. The paving of streets had begun in Italy as early as the thirteenth century, and by the sixteenth the main streets, at least, of most European cities were paved. No distinction was made between street and pavement, for the only traffic was pedestrian or horse. Carriages began to appear in the sixteenth century, and gradually, as wheeled traffic grew in volume, streets were straightened to accommodate it and provision made for pedestrians, making even clearer the distinction between rich and poor.

The hygiene of cities was even more neglected than the hygiene of persons. Travellers reported with monotonous regularity the disgusting conditions which they met, conditions which were no worse than those of their own cities but were seen with a fresh eye. The gradually increasing prohibition on keeping livestock within the city-walls probably increased the level of filth; the pig, that universal scavenger kept by most poor families, had been allowed to wander at will to find his own food. Excluded from the city, the task of street cleaning was left to dogs, rather more choosy in their diet. The streets were a dumping ground for every form of rubbish; only the fact that it was organic and sooner or later became a sludge saved the streets from becoming impassable. In the process of breaking down, it turned into a thick, oily, blue-black liquid which saturated the ground, stained walls all along their base and provided a fruitful breeding ground for disease. The practice of burying the dead within the city did nothing to lower the threshold of disease. The height of a cemetery would increase fourfold and more over the centuries; it would be located near the parish church

—and so would the common well. The gradual percolation of tainted water would find its way into the drinking supply with inevitable results. The fires which frequently swept through cities were the most efficient prophylactic known; without them, the crowded quarters of rich and poor alike would have become untenable.

THE VITRUVIAN CULT

The cities which entered the Renaissance were alike in one particular; they were growths whose size and shape developed according to local needs. The city wall alone was planned as a whole; within, only the size of a given building dictated the planning of a particular area. The cathedral accounted for a large site which might even incorporate a handful of streets and squares but elsewhere buildings appeared as they were needed, or were adapted from others. The very theory of overall planning was absent until the latter part of the fifteenth century when the work of a Roman architect, Vitruvius Polio, came again into circulation. Vitruvius had been an architect in Augustan Rome and his work, *De Architectura*, probably dates about 30 B.C. As an architect he was not of the first order but his book was the only text on the subject, which came into a world hungry for all that was classical. The re-discovery of architecture followed much the same lines as the re-discovery of geography; the ancient author supplied the impetus for minds more than capable of pursuing their own research. Men who believed that they were resurrecting Vitruvius were in fact using him to give order to their own theories. Essentially, Vitruvius treated a city as a complete unit which could, and should, be designed as a house is designed with all parts subordinate to the whole. Sanitation, roads, squares, public buildings, ratio of building sizes, all found their place. The first treatise based upon Vitruvius was by a Florentine, Leon Battiste Alberti, published in 1485, only thirteen years after his death. It was the first of a

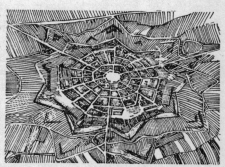

72 Palma Nova, Italy: the extreme in rigid town-planning

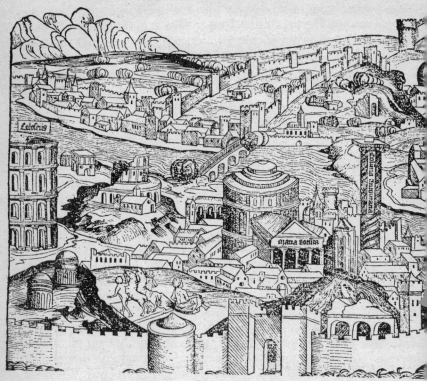

73 Panorama of Rome in 1493, showing old St Peter's (*at top*

long line of such works which stretched down to the nineteenth
century, exerting enormous influence. Most of these works were
beautifully, indeed, over-elaborately illustrated; given the mathematical basis of the cult it was perhaps inevitable that it should go
to extremes, a city being planned as though it were a geometric
problem without reference to the human and geographic elements.
Perfection of planning in theory led to a certain aridity in practice.

It is therefore perhaps fortunate that few cities were built
entirely upon the Vitruvian principle. Here and there local
necessity, usually military, demanded the establishment of a new
city and, occasionally, the whole could be built according to the
new theory, as with the case of Palma Nova in the Venetian state
(*72*). But, in general, architects had to be content with piecemeal

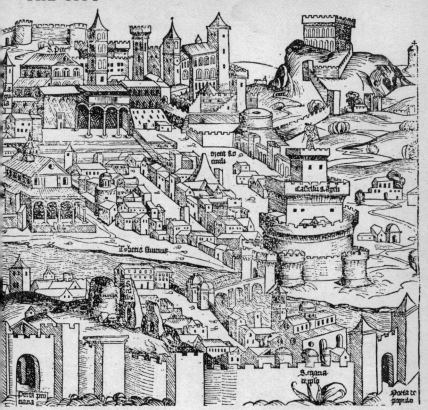

117)   *From a contemporary woodcut in Schedel's 'Weltchronik'*

development, as there were few opportunities for wholesale demolition and reconstruction. The kind of passive resistance the architect met with is well illustrated by the reception given to Leonardo da Vinci's proposal for satellite development around Milan. The great plague of 1484 had carried off 50,000 citizens and da Vinci wanted to establish ten new cities, housing 30,000 people in 5,000 houses, 'so as to separate this great congregation of people who herd together like goats ... filling each space with foul odour and sowing seeds of pestilence and death'. Nothing was done; there was neither financial profit nor military advantage to be gained and the Lord of Milan preferred to spend his money on the beautification of his own court. So throughout Europe; with one great exception the cities had already found their final form and there

117

was no space for large-scale planning. The one exception was Rome.

The first city of Christendom had fallen upon evil times during the Middle Ages, culminating in the removal of the Papacy to Avignon in 1305. For over a century there was no authority in the city strong enough to curb the ambitions of the great families and the almost bestial ferocity of the mob. The city mouldered while the other cities of Italy were increasing in beauty. The city of Augustus had been of a construction so solid as to defy the ravages of time and the attacks of barbarians; it was collapsing at the hands of its own citizens, partly

74 Decorating a building, 1465

through the destruction caused by faction warfare but mostly because the massive structures presented a source of ready-made building material. In 1443, however, the Great Schism ended and the Papacy was again established in Rome. It was Pope Nicholas V who first turned his attention to the appalling condition of the Eternal City, seeing that it must be virtually re-built 'so as to compel all to acknowledge her as the Capital of the World' (73). It was a gigantic task. The city had once housed a million people, the largest number brought permanently into one area until the nineteenth century: no other European city was to equal the size of Augustan Rome until the expansions following the Industrial Revolution. In 1377 it housed perhaps 20,000 people: the Seven Hills were abandoned, the population preferring to live in the unhealthy marshy area by the

118

Tiber; cattle wandered through the ruined streets; the great Forum itself lost its identity, became known merely as *Campo Vaccino*, the 'Cow Field'; animals remained where they died, adding their quota to the rotting materials underfoot. No city in Europe had fallen so low from so great a height.

From the time that Nicolas V planned his reconstruction to the year that Bernini added the great colonnaded approach to St Peter's over 160 years passed. The Popes who reigned during that century and a half varied from good to vile, from the scholarly Nicolas to the degenerate Alessandro Borgia. Yet they shared a passion which created the first of the Renaissance cities, a passion for art and architecture, a desire to make of the ancient city a seat which, admittedly reflecting their own glory, would yet be a fitting capital of Christendom. The names of the architects who worked there is a roll-call of fame; Alberti, the first of the Vitruvians, Bramante, san Gallo, Bernini, Raphael, Michelangelo, and others, overshadowed by these greater, who would yet have been the ornaments of lesser courts. Much that was done was regrettable: the demolition of the venerable St Peter's to make way for Bramante's new church caused a storm of protest. But the absolute authority of the Papacy was able to force through one of the great town-planning projects of history. The result was not merely a grandiloquent façade for a prince; some of the benefits spilled over for the common citizen to enjoy for the water-supply was improved, the ancient sewage system restored, the ever-present dangers of fire and plague pushed back a little further on his horizon.

URBAN LIFE

The city was a stage upon which was played out, in public view, many activities which today are conducted behind the privacy of walls. The details which struck the eye were astonishingly varied; the irregularity of the buildings, the eccentric variety and colour of costumes, the technical processes of innumerable trades carried on in the streets—all these gave the Renaissance city a colour lacking in the uniformity of a modern city. But at the same time there was a homogenity, a flowing and a mixing of groups which proclaimed the essential unity of the city. In the twentieth century the eye has become accustomed to the subdivisions created by the great growth of cities: pedestrians and vehicles move in different worlds; industry is segregated from commerce, and both are

75 Town traders, including clothier (*left*), barber (*centre*) and confectioner (*right*)

segregated from residential areas, which are themselves divided according to wealth. A citizen can pass his life without seeing a loaf of bread being baked or a dead man being buried. The larger the city becomes, the more the citizen becomes separated from his fellows until the paradox of loneliness in the midst of great crowds becomes a commonplace.

In a walled city of perhaps 50,000 people, the majority of whose homes were small cabins, lack of space encouraged the existing preference to live out life in public. The shopkeeper sold his wares from what was virtually a stall; the shutters of the ground-floor windows were hinged to come down, forming a shelf or table (75). He and his family still lived in the upper rooms of the house; only with increasing wealth was he able to maintain an independent shop with assistants, and himself live in open suburbs. The master craftsman also used the lower room of his house as a workshop (51), sometimes displaying his goods for sale on the spot. Craftsmen or tradesmen were gregarious: every city had its Weavers' Lane, its Butchers' Row, its Fishmongers' Alley, and if there were not room enough within the tiny, crowded rooms, or if the weather were fine, then the craftsmen moved out on to the street, making it indistinguishable from a market-place. Dishonest men paid the penalty in the public square, even as they earned their living in the public street. Pilloried, they would be fittingly punished with defective wares burnt at their feet or hung around their neck; a vintner selling bad wine was forced to drink a quantity of it and the rest was poured over him; a fishmonger was obliged to endure the stench of rotten fish or have it rubbed over face and hair.

The city at night knew a profound silence and darkness. Even where a compulsory curfew was not in force, the wise man was off the streets and safely behind his barred doors by nightfall. The man who was discovered abroad during the night hours by the officers of the city had to be prepared to give a very convincing reason for his eccentric activity. There was nothing to tempt the honest man to leave his home, for public entertainments ceased with sunset and most private persons pursued the frugal habit of going to bed with the sun. Tallow candles were available but were highly expensive; even the evil-smelling dips of material soaked in fat were economically used, for the fat cost more than meat. A working day which ran from dawn to dusk left little energy for carousel at night. The reading of the Bible, appearing now in many homes as the printing presses got into their stride; a little music for those who could afford an instrument—lute or viol or flute, singing for those who could not; conversation; this was how the vast mass of people must have spent the brief period between the evening meal and bed.

But the lack of entertainment at night was more than compensated by that provided, at the public expense, by day. The frequent holy days of the Church reduced the number of working days each year to a figure probably even lower than that

76 A religious procession

existing today. The fast days were rigorous, and backed by the power of the law but the feast days were taken as literally; they were not only parts of a liturgy but days of active rejoicing. On these days the unity of the city was made visible in the great public processions to the church (76). Spectators were few, for most were participants. Albrecht Dürer witnessed such a procession in Antwerp, his artist's eye delighting in the moving pattern of colour and shape. It was on the Feast of the Assumption,

and the whole town of every craft and rank were assembled, each dressed in his best according to his rank. And all ranks and guilds had their sign, by which they might be known. In the intervals, great costly pole-candles were borne, and three long old Frankish trumpets of silver. There were also in the German fashion many pipes and drummers. All the instruments were loudly and noisily blown and beaten. . . . There were the Goldsmiths, the Painters, the Masons, the Broderors, the Sculptors, the Joiners, the Carpenters, the Sailors, the Fishermen, the Clothmakers, the Bakers, the Tailors, the Cordwainers, indeed, workmen of all kind and many craftsmen and dealers who work for a living. After these came the shooters with guns, crossbows, and the horsemen and foot-soldiers also. Before them however went all the religious orders. . . . A very large company of widows also took part; they support themselves with their own hands and observe a special rule. They were dressed from head to foot in white garments made expressly for the occasion, very sorrowful to see. . . . Twenty persons bore the image of the Virgin Mary with the Lord Jesus, adorned in the costliest manner. In this procession very many delightful things were shown, most splendidly got up. Wagons were drawn along with masques upon ships and other structures. Behind them came the Company of the Prophets in their order, and scenes from the New Testament. . . . From the beginning to the end the procession lasted more than two hours before it had gone past our house.

The delightful things 'splendidly got up', which so impressed Dürer in Antwerp, would have entranced him in Florence or Venice, for the Italians developed the religious festival as a form of art. On the Feast of Corpus Christi in Viterbo in 1482, the entire route of the procession was divided into sections, each the responsibility of a cardinal or high prelate. Each rivalled the other in decorating his section with costly drapings, providing each with a stage upon which a mystery was enacted, so that the whole showed a series of plays on the death and resurrection of Christ. The stage used in Italy for the Mysteries followed the general European pattern: it was a structure in three sections, the lower and upper serving as Heaven and Hell and the main platform as Earth (77). The great attraction was the elaborate machinery which enabled the actors to appear as if they floated through the air. There was one in Florence which consisted of a suspended globe, surrounded by angels, out of which a car would appear and descend to Earth. Leonardo da Vinci prepared an even more elaborate machine for the Sforzas which showed the

77   Stage for Mystery play

movements of the heavenly bodies, each carrying its tutelary spirit.

The secular processions in Italy took both their name and form from the great Triumphs of classical Rome. They were organised sometimes to honour a visiting prince or victorious general, sometimes for their own sake. The great names of Rome were resurrected, dressed in toga and laurel wreath and sent again in chariots through the city. Allegory was the keynote: Faith overcame Idolatry, Virtue destroyed Vice; the condition of man was shown in his Three Ages; every human and supernatural situation was made concrete and set in motion. The Italians did not trouble to develop the literary content of their scenes, preferring to lavish expense upon the visual impact, and the allegorical figures are two-dimensional, stiff creations which speak pompous lines without conviction and move off for the next spectacle. But the splendour which the eye perceived was sufficient. In no other city of Europe could civic pride find more brilliant expression than the annual ritual of marrying the sea which took place in Venice. It was a curious mixture of commercial arrogance, Christian gratitude and

78　The Bucentaur of Venice

Oriental symbolism, originating in A.D. 997 when the then Doge
poured a libation into the main seaway before advancing to
battle. On every Ascension Day thereafter the victory was cele-
brated. The great state barge called the Bucentaur was rowed to the
same point and there the Doge cast a ring into the sea, proclaiming
his city's espousal to the element which had made it great (78). On
all civic occasions the Bucentaur dominated: where processions
in other cities moved through dust and heat, the Venetians glided
down their great water high-road. The Bucentaur was developed
from the fighting galley which had swept the Adriatic clean of
Venice's enemies. It possessed still the wicked ramming beak of
the fighting ship, but its upper deck was canopied with crimson and
cloth of gold; gold-leaf over its length made it blaze in the sun and
at its bow was a life-size figure of Justice, wielding sword and scales.
Visiting princes would be conveyed to the island city on this state
barge, escorted by countless smaller craft garlanded and decorated
with rich hangings, and brought to the very door of their lodgings.
Little wonder that the Venetian carnivals, organised with the same
splendid disregard for expense, the same lusty, almost barbaric

love of colour, should attract visitors from all over Europe. The population of the city would double at these times. It was probably from Venice that the fashion of the masquerade spread through the courts of Europe. Other Italian cities introduced the use of masked players in their Mysteries but it was the Venetian, pleasure-loving behind his commercial acumen, who saw the value of the mask as a piquant addition to the Carnival.

The military sports of the Middle Ages continued with little change, save that some moved down through society as when the Fishmongers of Nuremberg organised their own tourney. Archery competitions seem to have increased with popularity even as the bow as a weapon was disappearing from the battlefield. But the most popular festivals were still those whose roots were in pre-Christian Europe. The Church, having failed to uproot them, had baptised some but others still continued, in Catholic and Protestant country alike, in their unchanging form. The greatest of these was May Day, the pagan welcome to spring (79). Rich and poor alike still rode or walked out of the city to bring in the blossom, and the day was devoted to dancing and feasting. To be Lord of the May was a costly honour, for to him fell the expenses of the celebration; men were

79 May Day festivities

known to flee the city rather than accept. The festival brought back into the city something of that countryside which was never far distant. All through Europe the rhythm of the seasons found expression in these folk festivals; they varied in detail and name from locality to locality, but their family resemblance was strong. The Lord of Misrule still reigned on one day in winter, descendant of the Roman Saturnalia which in its turn was a prehistoric survival marking the turning of the year. Suppressed again and again, he yet appeared in local festivities, with the Clown, the Swordsman and those masked dancers whose first representation is in cave art. Millennia old, the festivities yet found a natural place in cities where the thump of the printing press and the rattle of the carriage wheel betokened a new world.

THE TRAVELLER

The major cities of Europe were linked by reasonably efficient postal systems. The common citizen was free to take advantage of them—provided that he was prepared to have his mail read; the authorities who operated the systems were as interested in espionage as they were in communication. In spite of the appalling condition of the roads, traffic was increasing. The great wave of pilgrimages had reached its climax and was now receding, but in its place came companies of merchants, busier than ever with the increase of trade; state officials were ubiquitous and the tramp and clatter of soldiers on the march never ceased. The private traveller was no longer rare; men like the restless Erasmus moved from one centre of learning to another seeking a livelihood. Some even travelled for the purpose of education, if not actively for pleasure and, in Italy, there arose a whole new school of topographic writers who guided the curious to places of interest. Most men travelled on horseback but, here and there, appeared the coach (80), reputed to

80 German coach of 1563. (For cross-country journeys at least four horses would be required)

have been invented in Kotze or Kocs in Hungary. The majority of these vehicles must have been used for show, for they provided little comfort. The bodywork was swung upon straps, which, theoretically acting as springs, in practice transformed the motion into a nauseating plunging and swaying. Their average speed was perhaps 20 miles per day, depending upon the conditions of the road, and each required at least six horses to drag it through the mud of winter. They were vulnerable to the frequent pitfalls in the road; on one stretch of road in Germany three were wrecked in the same great hole which also claimed the life of a wretched peasant.

The Roman roads still formed the main arteries of Europe but even these magnificent structures could not withstand the depredations of the peasantry. A man wishing to build a byre or even a cottage would quite naturally turn to the ready-hewn, plentiful supply of stone which the road represented. Once the upper layers were removed, the weather and traffic did the rest, for in few localities were there any ordinances which governed the maintenance of roads outside the cities. In England, a miller who needed clay for repairs dug a hole ten feet across and eight feet deep. It filled with water and a traveller fell in and was drowned. Charged, the miller pleaded that he had no intention of causing death and claimed that he had no other source for his clay. He was freed. Ancient custom, however, prescribed the minimum width of the road; here it had to allow the passage of two wagons side by side; there a knight must be able to ride with his lance held sideways. In France, the Roman roads which ran through forests were increased from their average width of 20 feet to some 78 feet, as a measure of protection against bandits. These latter increased as the rich traffic multiplied and the wise man travelled in a company of his fellows, all armed. The lone traveller was an object of suspicion and was likely to find himself in the local prison until he could give good reason for being in that area.

Journeys across Europe, even under the best circumstances, might take weeks. The inn therefore achieved a prime importance (81). It could be a huge establishment, as with the great inn called 'The Ox', at Padua, which had stabling for 200 horses; it could be a tiny, evil-smelling tavern on the wayside. Those in lonely areas were frequently traps for the unwary; an Austrian innkeeper was proved to have murdered over 185 guests over a period of years, amassing a large treasure in the process. But most contemporaries

81   The main room of a wayside inn

give a friendly enough picture of the innkeeper; the good lady whom William Caxton used for his model in one of the first handbooks for travellers must have seemed very welcoming at the end of a weary day's travel. Caxton printed his handbook in 1483; it provided his monoglot fellow-countrymen with French phrases which would at least enable them to find a way out of the city, hire a horse, and obtain a bed for the night. The conversation at the inn was courteous rather than comprehensive, but it brings to life a situation which was repeated every night in some city in Europe. 'Dame, god be here. Felaw, ye be welcome. May I have a bed withinn? Ye[a], well and clenly, [even if] were ye alle twelve. Nay, but we thre. Is there to ete? Ye, ynough, god be thanked. Brynge it to us, gyve hey to the horse and straw them well.' The travellers eat, prudently check the price of the meal, and ask that it be added to the morrow's reckoning. Then 'Brynge us to sleep; we ben weary. Jenette, light the candell, and lede them there above in the [upper] room; and bere them hot water for to wash their feet and cover them with quysshons.' This was evidently a superior inn. The travellers were waited upon at table and had obviously not brought their own food, as was a custom. They had a candle to light them to bed and hot water provided. Possibly, if they were very lucky, they might even have a bed apiece, instead of having to share one with strangers. But even whether the inn was luxurious with entertainment provided, or merely a cabin against the city wall, the traveller could relax for a few hours, safe not only from the weather and wild animals, but also from his fellow man.

Chapter VI

THE VIOLENT WORLD

THE PLAGUE

SHORTLY after the beginning of the sixteenth century, there appeared a curious new series of drawings. They were, at first, drawn upon church walls but later appeared as woodcuts, heavily inked, intended to be carried on the person as a perpetual *memento mori* (*82, 108*). The dominant figure was Death, usually crowned, for he was king, leading in boisterous or stately dance the peoples of the Earth; Pope and beggar, Emperor and peasant, monk, usurer, saint, all briefly equal in ghastly revelry. The Dance of Death was French in origin, but spread swiftly to all the nations of Europe; priests had originated it to warn sinners; the laity took it up. Once they had sung of the prowess of hero, or knight, or lover, but now it was the prowess of Death. Towards the end of the century he abandoned his dance and appeared as a sudden visitor come to take the lover from his mistress, the usurer from his money bags, the farmer from his field. But whether as leader of a dance or arresting sergeant, he dominated, sometimes as a grinning skeleton, sometimes as a ravaged body, but always human, man using his own form as terrible warning, 'Once I was as you, soon you shall be as I'.

The preoccupation with death arose out of the plague, the disease which hovered over Europe for four centuries, carrying off scores of thousands. Chronicler after chronicler recorded the same appalling pictures in Italy, France, Germany, Spain, the Low

82   Dance of Death

Countries, in every century from the fourteenth to the eighteenth: streets littered with dead; cities empty save for the gangs of grave diggers, silent save for the tinkle of their bells. Society again and again seemed to crumble under the blow so that savage customs arose and throve—cannibalism, murder, sorcery; laws broke down for there were none to administer them; 'the dead outnumber the living so that it is scarcely possible to bury them'—this phrase was repeated again and again. The accounts exaggerate, but not greatly, and it is possible to check the degree of exaggeration, for the plague continued in other parts of the world down to the nine-teenth century, and observations made under scientific conditions have substantiated much of the contemporary reports of earlier centuries. The speed with which death could follow an attack—usually within three days, sometimes within twenty-four hours; the velocity with which it increased to a peak, like a fire feeding upon itself; the level of mortality which was at least 55 per cent of those attacked—all these are matters of fact. Even the sum of the numbers who died are in proportion with that which occurred under modern observed conditions. The Black Death of 1347-8 carried off one third of the population of Europe. This was a pandemic, sweeping across Europe in one period; the subsequent epidemics were limited in extent but were as virulent in effect; one half, three quarters, sometimes the whole population of a thriving city or village would be carried off.

The word 'plague' was often used of any unidentified epidemic but usually it was limited in meaning to either pneumonic or bubonic plague, a disease of rodents which was transmitted to humans by fleas. In the former, the most lethal of the two, the lungs became inflamed; in the latter, great painful swellings called buboes appeared on the body, usually in the groin and armpit. The Black Death took its vivid name from one of the symptoms—haemorrhage spots which were crowded closely together and, after death, took on a dark hue. The cause was for long believed to be supernatural. Its coming could be told by portentous signs—comets, earthquakes and apparitions. The Plague Virgin stalked, a hideous counterpart to the goddess Flora; in place of flowers she sprinkled plague poison. The Devil himself makes an appearance, knocking at those doors where Death would later enter. Some believed that the disease was caused by the exhalation of evil people. A contributory factor to the belief in supernatural causes was the apparent capriciousness of the disease. It obeyed a periodic law, mounting steadily to a peak in spite of prophylactics, then dropping away even though conditions favoured its continuance.

This law was its only constant factor. In general, it flourished in insanitary conditions during the

83   Plague sufferers in front of a church

summer months, a temperature of 80 degrees being most favourable. But the exceptions to this were almost as frequent as the rule. The great plague of Moscow and the Volga Basin raged in the depths of a Russian winter; the comparatively sanitary cities of Italy suffered as greatly as the filthy cities of England; Alpine villages were no more immune than the villages of marsh or plain. A village or town could be virtually destroyed while its neighbour a few miles away was untouched. The reason was that the disease would lie dormant for months or even years in certain areas which provided a permanently favourable condition; it would rise again and provide a source of infection whence other places would be contaminated by travellers. Even here, the degree of contagion appears capricious: a French physician deliberately donned the shirt of a plague patient and wore it without ill effect for two days. In Egypt two criminals were for the sake of experiment placed in the bed and clothes of plague patients. Both took the disease but only one died. The degree of contagion depended upon the length of time the disease was abroad. The draconian habit of immuring all the members of a family within their home was not only tantamount to a death sentence upon them, but caused a fatal concentration of the poison, making of the house a pestilential reservoir.

The only certain medicine for a healthy person was to flee the city. 'Quick, far and late', was the formula: 'Start quick, go far, delay return till late'. It was the invariable habit adopted by the wealthy. Princes laid down the most rigorous quarantine zones, forbidding their subjects to approach under penalty of death. Administration collapsed with the absence of the court and the hapless inhabitants of the city were left to be the prey of the violent. For not all could escape; the very rich could afford to leave, the very poor had no ties. But in between was the vast mass of people without resources save their trade, forced to choose between braving the plague at home or wandering like animals in the country. Even then there was no absolute safety for both wild and domestic animals died of the plague, their bodies creating another source of contagion. For those who, perforce, stayed at home to follow their trade there were a score of 'remedies', some disgusting, some supernatural, some with a hint of practicability—but all useless.

It was commonly held that the air itself was a breeding ground, that the atmosphere was thick and vitiated. If it could only be set in motion, all would again be well. To that end, bells were rung, firearms shot off, loud music played. New milk and warm bread, small birds and spiders were all believed to be capable of absorbing the poison and were placed in rooms before people entered. The principle of disinfectant lay behind the use of pungent herbs burnt to release their odours: fir, laurel, oak leaves, wormwood, lavender, marjoram were all employed. These, though breathtaking enough, were at least pleasant to smell, but the principle was carried to ludicrous extremes when actual stenches were believed to be even more effective. Leather and horn were burnt, stinking billygoats tethered indoors, even human ordure was used to combat evil with evil. Some doctors protested. 'I cannot conceive what benefit can be derived from this. How could such a stench prove beneficial to them? Quite on the contrary, I believe that such poisonous stinks are rather the cause of more infections; some nevertheless believe that a certain town in Holland owes its immunity from the plague solely because of its piggish filth.' For the delicate stomached, there was the apothecary who, for a stiff fee, would provide a regimen. On Sunday, the patient was to smell essence of rue, roses, cloves, all contained in a small box of juniper or aloe. On Monday the apothecary provided boxes containing green rue, wormwood, rosemary, thyme; on Tuesday, juniper placed on a sponge—and so through the week, a different combination every day. The pomander, consisting of a ball of resin or amber stuffed with cloves, was very popular. Tobacco was deemed particularly valuable, whether smoked in pipes or used as snuff.

The apothecaries made a good living and, though they did little good, they at least introduced a pleasant smell into evil-smelling rooms (*84*). More dubious were those who supplied magical or holy remedies against the plague. Amulets were a common feature of life in ordinary times, protecting the wearer from this or that stroke of misfortune. In periods of plague their manufacture and sale rose astonishingly. Some were exotic; the bezoar stone, the unicorn's horn and certain precious stones, particularly the amethyst, were available only to the wealthy. The poor made do with a bone from the head of a toad, tongues of venomous snakes, or hollowed hazelnuts filled with mercury. They turned to the Church not only for spiritual comfort but also practical remedy, and the Church was swift to oblige. The wearing of a paper with the Holy Names, together with the reciting of specified prayers was infallible. 'He who does this shall not die of the plague for it has been tried many times where the plague prevailed.' Those who died were judged lacking in faith. Pieces of paper, inscribed with a prayer, folded seven times, and eaten every day on an empty stomach, was another certain remedy. The citizens of Naples possessed a letter written to them by the Mother of God in which perpetual immunity was promised. It diffused a sweet smell for ten miles around, but later proved ineffectual

84   Doctor visits a plague patient
From a medical textbook of 1493

85 Hospital: the doctor carries a pomander for protection (*see also 84*)

when Naples suffered the worst epidemic in recorded history with a death-roll of 300,000 in five months.

One of the few effective measures was that of quarantine. The Venetian regulations evolved between 1348 and 1485 formed the pattern for others to follow. The fact that Venice was an island immensely assisted the authorities; the fact that it was a port made such regulations vital. Many a devastating epidemic had been introduced by ship. The Venetian authorities confined all immigrants to one of the islands for a period of forty days, a period of religious significance, for it was the length of time in which Christ sojourned in the wilderness. A sanitary council was established which, in 1504, was given powers of life and death; bills of health were introduced in 1527. Other countries followed suit with a mixture of practical and religious controls. Wherever the plague struck violently enough, laws were sure to be enacted with the intention of suppressing immorality; the playing of dice, gambling generally and drunkenness were the usual activities attacked. Dice manufacturers, faced with the loss of livelihood, turned to making rosary beads for which there was a steady demand.

In 1533 the Parlement of Paris issued a lengthy ordinance relating to public hygiene. All plague sufferers and those who came into contact with them were to carry a white wand. The heirs of those who died from the plague were forbidden to remove property from the house until the epidemic had abated. The public bathing establishments were closed. Surgeons were forbidden to treat ordinary patients after treating plague sufferers, and the blood they drew was not to be thrown into the river. The duty of every citizen was to ensure that the road in front of his dwelling was washed down twice a day and the gutters cleared. In Troyes, there was an absolute prohibition against entering the town. Four old women who did so, in order to sell old clothes, were whipped out of the town at the cart's tail. Whole streets were closed by chains in Berlin and a guard set upon them—turning them into cemeteries. Punishment for infringement of these regulations went even beyond death. In Königsberg a maidservant infected herself and her master through taking articles from a house struck by plague. She died, but when her crime was discovered her body was exhumed, hung from the gallows and afterwards burnt. But controls over limited areas for limited periods could have little long term effect. Without an adequate sewage system, water supply, or widespread quarantine there was little to be done save to pray and bury the dead.

A peculiarly horrible profession developed from the enormous death-roll (86). Normal decencies were abandoned as the plague reached its height and the dead were left to the mercies of professional grave-diggers. Their task included the collection of corpses, and the disgusting and dangerous nature of their work ensured that it was left to the dregs of society. Condemned prisoners would choose it, preferring distant to immediate death; liberated galley slaves were common, an adequate comment on the conditions

86 Burying the dead during the early stages of an epidemic; as the death-roll grew, communal burials became normal and the professional grave-digger came into his own

aboard these vessels. Death doubtless claimed many but conferred a temporary immunity upon the rest so that they became a hideous aristocracy in an inverted social order. The city was free to them for they had legal entry into every house where plague was suspected. Blackmail was added to the ordinary attractions of loot. There was nothing to prevent them declaring that a member of the household was infected; it was then their duty to drag such a person to the plague house. A man would give his all to prevent such an end for himself or his family. The grave-diggers' treatment of the dead was callous, but their treatment of the weak was evil. Out of malice or impatience they hastened the death of the sick or even carried them, still breathing, to the common grave. They were accused, with frequent justice, of deliberately spreading the plague by strewing infected matter about the city in order to prolong their own livelihood, or to drive the inhabitants from a house so that it could be looted. Plague-spreading was a common charge even against ordinary citizens and, if proved, incurred the most atrocious of deaths. Plague patients would deliberately seek out the healthy and attempt to transmit the infection, partly from malice, partly from the belief that in this way they could rid themselves of the disease. It was believed to be a weapon used by the new race of Protestants against true believers. In Lyons, in 1564, the authorities declared that: 'the heretics, when they saw the number of their adherents decreasing, had recourse to the children of Satan. With ointments received from Hell, they smeared the house of Catholics.' There never lacked scapegoats.

WITCHCRAFT

In the sixteenth and seventeenth centuries the cult of witchcraft assumed an importance which had been unknown during the so-called Dark Ages. Those same centuries which saw men examining the structure of the Universe, saw also the irrational cult of demons and ghosts take its final form. Paradoxically, it was the Christian Church which, seeking with all its powers to combat the practice of Satanism, gave that same practice a form. It was necessary to define witchcraft in order to combat it and, by so defining, the Church gave shape to what had been little more than folklore. The familiar elements had long been abroad in Europe before they were formally indicted, but for centuries the Church had been content to dismiss them as mere fantasy. The legend of the woman who flew by night came in for particular scorn. 'Who is such a fool that he believes that to happen in the body which is done only in the spirit?' Such sturdy common sense was forced at last to give ground before a rising fanaticism. In 1458 the ancient ban of the Church on such beliefs was broken by an inquisitor in Germany who argued that a new sect had grown up which even the Fathers of the Church had been unable to foresee. Twenty-six years later Pope Innocent VIII, alarmed at the alleged increase of the cult of witchcraft in Germany, opened a formal crusade against it and appointed two inquisitors, Kramer and Sprenger, to examine the whole structure. The pair devoted five years of labour and produced at last a textbook on witchcraft which, even to this day, is accepted by some as the corner stone of all legal action against witches.

The *Malleus Maleficarum* was cast in the form of a scholarly disputation; the case for each phenomenon was stated, the objections examined, and the conclusion made. It is difficult to perceive the character of Sprenger, the principal author: some see him as 'a dangerous and evil-minded fanatic who revels in the preposterous and even more in the sensual'; others hold as firmly that he was a man of immense learning and piety, contributing what he could to the eradication of a damnable cult. Certainly his work bears the impression of deep thought and careful examination. But he is absorbed to morbidity with that sexual aspect of witchcraft which dominated the judgment of his contemporaries, discussing at great length and detail whether infants may be generated by demons through human beings. It was Sprenger, too, who was responsible for one of the great slanders upon women.

87   A witch and the Devil
Early sixteenth-century woodcut

137

Witchcraft, he asserted, was more natural to them than to men because of the inherent wickedness of their hearts, and because of their greater love of carnality, 'and all this is indicated by the etymology of the word for *femina* comes from *fe* (faith) and *minus*, since she is ever weaker to hold and preserve the Faith'. That conclusion was to bring about the agony of untold numbers of women, most of them old and feeble-minded. Men were to burn in their hundreds, but women burnt in their thousands.

The demonology which obsessed Europe for over two centuries was built up partly by deduction but mostly from the confessions of witches themselves. Ideally, the witch should confess spontaneously, yet 'it is lawful at times to proceed on the strength of the indubitable indications and conjectures'. In other words, if the witch proved unforthcoming with vivid details, then the prosecutor could supply them from the wealth of scholastic studies at his disposal, adding other details as his own imagination dictated. The witch nearly always confessed to the most preposterous accusations and another body of picturesque details was added to the store. Torture was an inherent, and legal, part of the proceedings and few human beings could accept the prospect of suffering which would end only in death. Counsel, if allowed, was chosen by the prosecutor but was himself liable to be charged with witchcraft if he showed himself over-zealous in defence. The probability was that most of these so-called advocates were themselves but an arm of the prosecution. In certain Burgundian trials the nobleman, de Beauffort, who was accused was urged by his interrogator to confess. When de Beauffort protested, saying that it would be perjury to confess to something that he had not done, he was promised absolution in advance. He at length confessed—and was promptly condemned.

The questions of the inquisitors naturally fell into a pattern, for they commenced with a preconceived idea; equally naturally, the answers followed a similar pattern so that it did in fact appear that a new cult, complete down to the last horrifying detail, had sprung up all over Europe. Under torture the accused confessed and implicated others—who were tortured and implicated yet more in an ever-widening circle. 'Christendom seemed to have grown delirious and Satan might well smile at the tribute to his power in the endless smoke of the holocaust which bore witness to the triumph of the Almighty.' Yet, from the first, there was sober opposition. A member of the Spanish Inquisition gave his considered opinion that the witch-hunters were themselves largely responsible for the growth of the cult. 'In the diseased state of the public mind every agitation of the matter is harmful and increases the evil. There were neither witches nor bewitched until they were talked about.' Silence and restraint were the best weapons. A result of this cool appraisal was that neither the practice nor the persecution of witchcraft achieved the same level in Spain as it did in the rest of Europe. All other countries contributed their quota to the growing mythology. The Germans emphasised the peculiar horror of the Sabbath, the French and Italians contributed the blasphemy of the Black Mass, England introduced the concept of the animal familiar, Sweden the human steed, shod like a horse, which conveyed witches to this Sabbath. That there were practising witches among those condemned there can be little doubt. Some may have been self-deluded—references to intoxicating drugs of one kind or another were frequent. Others may have been practising a genuine, non-Christian but not necessarily evil cult and were caught up in the general condemnation. But the majority were

88   Preparation for the Sabbath: on the right, a witch is being anointed with the magic salve

indulging in a common human desire for the esoteric, the desire to be a member of an exclusive group with secret language and rituals and the ability to enjoy, within that group, the brief exercise of power.

It was around the Sabbath that the great legends of witchcraft were woven (*88–9*). As a matter of common practice the meeting of witches called the Sabbath would be held only a little distance from the community where the witches dwelt. Civilisation stopped at the village or city limits; at night time the country beyond would be a black wilderness, covered still with primeval forests in many parts of Europe. It would be necessary to go only a few miles, perhaps only a few hundred yards beyond the dwellings to find absolute privacy. The occasional benighted traveller would be in no mood to linger and investigate strange lights or sounds for the very earthy fear of robbers would be as great a deterrent as fear of supernatural beings. Nevertheless, popular fancy believed that the Sabbath was held at some unspecified but distant place, arrival at which required supernatural agencies for transportation. Much learned attention was given to this problem of nocturnal flight and most scholars agreed that it was achieved by means of a magic salve. The inquisitor at the Burgundian trials provided a horrified world with the ingredients of one of the salves—for, as with other magic practices, it differed from place to place. This salve was obtained by feeding stolen, consecrated wafers to toads which were then burnt; powder distilled from the bones of hanged men, together with the blood of newly-born infants were added to the mess. If the witch's hands and feet and a small staff were smeared with this, the owner would be whisked away over woods, mountains, rivers and lakes to arrive infallibly at the spot fixed upon for the Sabbath. The making of the salve touched at every point upon which witches were held in horror; the profanation of the Host, the association with dank creatures, grave robbing, child murder.

The Devil or a deputy was present at all Sabbaths and took many forms: the traditional, with horns, tail and talons; the human and, most frequently, the animal. Stripped of the supernatural overtones, the descriptions of this devil-animal make it clear that it was a masked man, dressed in the skin of an animal, enacting the ritual of some primitive religion. Descriptions of the activities of the Sabbath itself varied with the imaginative power of the

89 Witches' Sabbath
After an early sixteenth-century woodcut by Hans Baldung Grien

witch or her accusers: cannibalism, obscene dances, ghoulish feasts, blasphemous religious rites, all found their place. The food reflected the prevailing obscenity. 'All who have been honoured at the Devil's table confess that the banquets are so foul, either in appearance or smell, that they would easily cause nausea in the hungriest and greediest stomachs.' Even the wine was disgusting, bearing the appearance of thick, clotted blood and served in filthy vessels. Devotees who could voluntarily feast in this manner must have gone far in degradation. But, though it was the Sabbath which took the popular and scholarly imagination, it was the witch at home upon whom the whole ghastly edifice was erected for it was from her confessions that the world at large learnt of witchcraft. Most communities could point to at least one woman, usually advanced in years, around whom suspicion clung. Unsupported testimony could send her to the stake. A woman being taken ill, it was suggested that witchcraft might be the cause. She agreed, but when she was unable to give the name of a witch, a list of local suspects was read out to her. One name caught her attention and, after due formalities, that person was burnt. Anything could be laid to the charge of a local witch by her neighbours. 'For if any adversity, grief, sickness, loss of children, corn, or liberty happen to them, by and by they exclaim upon witches as if certain old women here on Earth must needs be the contrivers of all men's calamities.' So, by their thousands, all over Europe women were hanged, or burned, or drowned for imaginary misdeeds. There was an element of justice, if perverted, for a witch was executed only if she were believed to have caused death or injury by her black art. It was England which introduced the principle of executing a witch, not for causing harm, but simply for being a witch (91).

The pseudo-science of the witch-finder which flourished in England was based upon detection of familiars—personal demons, usually in animal form, who served the witch. In return for their service, the witch suckled them on her own blood, an operation which left a distinctive mark known as the devil's mark or teat. Old women living alone were particularly vulnerable, for the pets they kept came under suspicion and their physical deformities arising from age could easily enough be identified as the devil's mark by a zealous witch-finder. The virtuous joy of detecting a witch was supplemented by the incentive of a cash reward. The activities of such men as Matthew Hopkins in England, the self-styled Witch Finder General, are more reminiscent of a rat-catcher than a hunter of super-natural beings. The charge that he was lining his pockets at the expense of the community pene-trated even Hopkins' thick skin and he claimed that he

90 Matthew Hopkins with witches and familiars *From the title-page of his 'Discovery of Witches', 1647*

demands but 20s. a towne and doth sometimes ride 20 miles for that and hath no more for his charges thither and back again (and it may be stayes a weeke there) and finds there 3 or 4 witches, or if it be but one, cheap enough, and this is the great summe he takes to maintain his Companie and 3 horses.

He described at length the group of demons attending a witch in Essex while he was present (90). Their names were a curious mixture of the homely and the exotic; Holt was like a white kitten, Jarmar appeared as a fat, legless spaniel, Vinegar Tom as a greyhound with the head of an ox, Sack and Sugar, a black rabbit. He argued that the names were a sure evidence of supernatural origin for no man could have invented them. His method of inducing confession was by a crude form of third degree: the witch was kept awake for twenty-four hours in a bright light until her familiars, in despera-tion for sustenance, would brave the light and be seen. He omitted to explain why a supernatural creature needed physical sustenance

91 Multiple execution of witches in England. On the left others wait their turn behind bars; on the right the informer receives his reward

so desperately. The pin test was the final proof, for the witch was supposed to feel no pain if a pin were thrust into the devil's mark. Many an accused succumbed to this test even before the formal trial for the devil's mark could appear over vital organs and the pin resembled a rapier.

The last execution of a witch in Europe took place in Germany, the country where the outbreak had commenced. There can be no accurate assessment of the numbers of witches executed between the fifteenth and seventeenth centuries. One inquisitor boasted that he had despatched 800 in fifteen years; during the sixteenth century 7,000 perished in Trier; in one year 400 were burnt in Toulouse, 500 in Geneva, 600 in Bamberg. The English records, probably more accurate than most, estimate 1,000 between 1542 and 1736—and England was reputed tolerant. At the other extreme the figure of 100,000 has been estimated for Germany as a whole during the seventeenth century. It must have seemed, to an unbiased observer, that those whom plague and war spared were to be eliminated by the fear, malice or fantasticism of their next-door neighbours.

144

WAR

The wars of the Renaissance were fought by mercenaries. It was this, rather than the use of cannon, which distinguished them from their predecessors. The trend towards employing mercenaries had commenced long before, for, although the nuclei of the great armies which trampled up and down Europe during the Hundred Years War were feudal, the bulk was mercenary. The standing army came into being after the Renaissance. Superficially, there seems little distinction between a mercenary and a paid soldier, but the soldier was more amenable to discipline for he was paid, or hoped to be paid, in times of peace. As with all other aspects of social life, periods shade into one another so that all three classes of fighting men existed at the same time. Pockets of feudal militia were to be found all over the Continent and experiments had been made with the formation of standing armies. But the typical soldier of the period was the mercenary, the man who, for a fixed sum and limited period, contracted to serve an employer.

In the days of feudal armies, the populace of an invaded country suffered grievously enough in peace as well as war. 'War must feed war' was the dictum. Little provision was made for the tens of thousands of men forming the army; none was made for the scores of thousands who followed them. A Bavarian army was once estimated as consisting of 30,000 combatants with 130,000 camp followers of both sexes and all ages. A general, campaigning in the Low Countries, complained that he had provisions of sorts for only 40,000 men but there were 120,000 people with them. It was expected that the whole mob would live off the country, a euphemism which meant that the invaders would take what they wanted by force. It was a technique which drastically hampered the movement of an army; it could not retreat back along the route of its advance, for there was nothing to sustain it. A well-conducted army would take only food—and leave the peasantry to starve. An ill-conducted army would take everything it could lay its hands upon, for loot was a recognised source of payment. These conditions prevailed throughout the era of the mercenaries and became even worse. The ratio of camp-follower to fighting man increased, for the mercenary was essentially a nomad and what family life he enjoyed was in the camp. But far worse for the local inhabitants was the ubiquity of the mercenary and the total lack of control over him. A feudal army came into a country

92 Horse- and foot-soldiers in the late fifteenth century: the Battle of Fornovo, 1495

to fight a specific war; that war lost or won, the bulk of the army would return home and disperse. The mercenaries attached to it would move on to find another war; if they stayed they would be exterminated, for they would be in the minority.

The common people over whom those waves of invaders passed like an Act of God developed a technique of survival; everything valuable that could not be carried was hidden and the peasantry retreated to the nearest walled city. The dwellers of a country area were linked to their city by many ties; they could be called upon to serve in the militia, they paid taxes to the civic authority, their produce fed the citizens. In turn, many citizens had a stake in the country, whether it were a grand villa or small farm and in times of war made room for their country neighbours within the city. An invading army undertook a siege with the greatest reluctance. Disease would soon arise among the soldiers, camped as they were without adequate sanitary facilities; if dysentery spared them, hunger did not. Provisions in the immediate area would be rapidly exhausted and the army would melt away as the soldiers went further and further afield to find food. The beleagured citizens and peasants could afford to wait, cramped though they were. In time,

93   Bartolomeo Colleoni, *condottiere* in Venetian service
Detail from the equestrian statue by Andrea Verrocchio

94   (*overleaf*) The burning of Savonarola in the piazza at Florence
From a contemporary painting by an unknown artist

95   English soldiers storming a town
From a French illumination in the 'Chroniques d'Angleterre',
late fifteenth century
(British Museum Royal MS. 14 E. IV)

the army would pass on and the peasants could return to their homes, dig up their valuables, and take up where they had left off. All standing crops would have been devoured as though by locusts; the physical passage of the vast mob would have trampled a swathe across the country, and there would be a certain amount of purely malicious damage. But with the knowledge that months, or even years, might elapse before the next invasion, the people of city and country were encouraged to repair the damage, sow new crops and establish normality.

The advent of the mercenaries destroyed this hard but clear-cut pattern. There were neither militia nor feudal levies to oppose them and they therefore remained in an area until richer spoils promised elsewhere. Conditions in peace-time were, if anything, far worse for the populace than conditions in war. Battles did at least require the presence of the mercenary and his employer would have to make some attempt to pay him. In peace-time mercenaries were the responsibility of no man and they consequently became bandits. Some of their leaders were men of high professional ability (93) who insisted upon a modicum of discipline in their Company, for discipline implied efficiency and efficiency could command more money. But the kind of man who turned mercenary was usually a mediocre soldier, preferring to extort gold from the helpless rather than to engage in battle with equals. He was of dubious value to his employer for he owed his allegiance first to himself and then to the captain of his Company. These captains were at the mercy of their followers, retaining their loyalty only so long as they could provide rich pickings. Battles between armies composed of mercenary companies were relatively bloodless and inconclusive. It was quite usual for a mercenary, taken prisoner, to agree to bear arms for his late employer's enemy. 'We have captured so many mercenaries', a general reported to his prince, 'that we can now fill the gaps in our own army.' The people of an area they were engaged to defend were no more exempt from their attentions than the people of the enemy's territory. Each locality had its tale of horror to tell, differing only in detail (97). The *Strasburger Zeitung* reported that a company of Poles, 'bloodthirsty and evil people', had entered Vienna.

In passing through a certain place they had chanced upon a wedding celebration, had cut down the bridegroom and wedding guests, violated the women, looted all the table and silverware, stripped the women of their clothes and carried off the bride. Outside the city here they are now selling for seven or eight gulden clothes which could not be made for a hundred thaler. The very horseboys have silver bowls out of which I have seen them drinking.

There was no adequate force to deal with these human wolves. By the time a volunteer group of sufficient strength could gather, the Company might be miles away. Isolated mercenaries could expect a painful death at the hands of an enraged populace but there was little that could be done against a band of men, several thousand strong, whose main talent was murder.

The rise of the mercenaries was largely the responsibility of the cities. In Italy and Germany particularly, the growing prosperity of the mercantile cities made it economically sensible to hire men to do the fighting. At the same time that very prosperity created rivalry, making wars ever more frequent so that even more soldiers were required. As Europe turned from an economy based on land in favour of one based on gold, so more ready money became available to hire soldiers. Princes were forced to follow the trend. The feudal ties were weakening even as princely ambitions were increasing. The Reformation added wars of religion, giving a new impetus to ancient hatreds. There was ample work for the mercenary.

96   Armourers at work

The first cannon was probably used on the battlefield of Crécy in 1346 and handguns and grenades were in use over most of Europe by the middle of the fourteenth century (95). But over a century passed before the use of gunpowder altered the basic pattern of warfare and it was not until

152

97 Mercenaries sacking a village   *From Holinshed's 'Chronicles', 1577*

98   Suit of armour, 1550

1 Crest	10 Vambrace
2 Skull	11 Gauntlet
3 Visor	12 Breast
4 Beavor	13 Taces
5 Gorget	14 Tassets
6 Shoulder-	15 Breech
guards	16 Cuisses
7 Pauldrons	17 Knee-cops
8 Rerebraces	18 Jambs
9 Elbow-cops	19 Solerets

the late sixteenth century that an adequate, personal firearm was developed. Spear, sword and bow continued to be used side by side with the new weapons and the mounted men-at-arms, each encased in plate armour weighing perhaps 350 lb., remained the hard core of armies until the sixteenth century. The Golden Age of armour, indeed, commenced fifty years after the first feeble cannon-shot at Crécy (96). Armour was tested by the most powerful weapon likely to be directed against it, and some suits still bear the 'proving mark' of a bullet. A contemporary observed that Sir Philip Sidney, killed in 1586, would have survived the battle had he not removed his thighpiece. There were at least nineteen main parts of a suit of armour (98), so contrived to give as much freedom of movement as possible while allowing maximum defence. But the most cunning armourer could do nothing about the great weight of metal necessary for defence. The wearer of one of the heavier suits had to be hoisted by crane on to the back of his horse, his enormous lance fitted to him, and there he stayed until unhorsed or the battle ended. In close proximity to several hundred of his fellows he formed part of a shock weapon almost impossible to withstand.

A squadron of men-at-arms was intended to clash with its opposite number in the enemy army. Weight alone was the criterion, the function of the great lance being to transmit the thundering momentum of armoured horse and rider and hurl the enemy to the ground. There he was as helpless as a turtle upon its back and could be despatched by the infantry or held to ransom.

The infantry in most European armies was a despised rabble in the Middle Ages; nevertheless, it was this same rabble who learnt at last how to withstand the shock of an armoured charge. The technique was developed by the Swiss. In their poor, mountainous country there was neither money to maintain, nor reason to employ, cavalry, and the horse did not possess for them the almost mystical attraction it possessed for other nations. They developed their own sturdy infantry and the weapon they used to oppose the onset of cavalry was the oldest in the world—the shaft tipped with a sharp point. In its new form it was called the pike, sometimes reaching as much as 18 feet in length (99). Closely grouped together, a mass of pikemen formed an almost impenetrable hedge of bristling steel points. Once the momentum of attack was lost, the man on horseback lost much of his menace. He still towered over the man on foot and could do great damage with his sword but another weapon was produced to overcome his remaining advantage. This was the halberd, a species of spear with the addition of a hook and axe upon the shaft. The hook was used to pluck at the knight, and

99　Pikemen. Cheap to produce and impregnable when massed, the
pike gave the foot-soldier the advantage

secure a hold; he was then dragged to the ground and speared or hacked to death.

The advantage passed from cavalier to infantryman with this weapon and the lumbering, metalclad horseman became a thing of the past. But the horse itself, with its superior speed and manoeuvrability and its advantage in height, remained a most valuable weapon, and cavalry swiftly adapted itself to the new conditions. It was immensely helped by personal firearms. The enormous weight of cannon limited its use to fixed points, usually during a siege, but the handgun could be developed for use on a battlefield. In its earliest form it was merely a tube mounted on a pole, the charge being ignited by a match. This was a three-yard length of cotton cord, soaked in saltpetre, and kept constantly alight and brought to the touch-hole by hand. Later, a mechanism was developed which brought the smouldering match into contact with the priming powder by means of a lever action. From this single weapon developed the arquebus (*100*) and musket (*101*) which, in conjunction with the pike, dominated European battlefields for two centuries, and the pistol which gave the horseman equality in firing power. The musketeer faced a peculiar hazard for he was obliged to carry upon his person a length of smouldering match in proximity to quantities of powder. Many a man blew himself up before he was even able to charge his piece. Charging was a complicated task. Black powder was held in one flask, finer priming powder in another. A measure of powder, together with a bullet taken from a leather bag, was rammed home, priming powder placed in the pan and ignited. It became customary to carry ready-measured charges of powder in little wooden boxes called patrons,

100   Arquebusier
From a sixteenth-century drill manual

and in the late sixteenth century musketeers carried bandoliers from which hung small wooden cylinders, each holding a measure of shot and powder, the forerunner of the cartridge. The musket itself was immensely long and could not be used without a support, and the equipment of a musketeer therefore included a heavy crutch for this purpose.

THE INQUISITION

There had existed for over 300 years an organisation specifically charged with the maintenance of Catholic orthodoxy in Europe. It had declined in power under the humanist popes of the early Renaissance

101 Musketeer, early seventeenth century

but the sixteenth century saw its resurgence. In some nations its power merged with the lay power of the sovereign; in others, in Spain and Italy particularly, it was a weapon wielded exclusively by the Church. Its terms of reference were wide; now it was the Jews who felt its power; now Muslims; now Christian heretics. Even an infringement of minor laws of the Church could bring a person before the tribunal: a drunkard could find himself awaiting trial with a simonite, a murderer or a blasphemer. And again and again the awesome power of the Inquisition was used as a means of private revenge, for it needed only a denunciation to set the wheels in motion.

It was in Spain that the Inquisition adopted its most terrifying form, achieving a degree of independence and ferocity which horrified even the Vatican. Established in 1478, it lingered on into the nineteenth century, long after other nations had discarded it.

That same country which, in a civilised manner, declined to prosecute witches, entered into an orgy of violence when prosecuting fellow-Christians, as well as Jews and Muslims. But though the violence in Spain was extreme, the methods employed were similar in all countries. In each town where it was decided to hold an inquisition an 'Edict of Faith' was promulgated, requiring all who knew of heresy to come forward and denounce it. It was a standing invitation for the discharge of private grudges, for the name of accusers was never made known to the defendant. He was imprisoned at his own expense and, even in the unlikely event of being found totally innocent, he was still fined—for the Inquisition could never be wrong. Before the evidence was made known to

him he was required to swear that he would never divulge the details of his 'trial'. In this manner the tribunal not only protected itself but also increased the fear in which it was held. A wise man, freed from its clutches, kept a very tight guard upon his tongue, leaving his friends and neighbours to imagine what they would. The judicial procedure of the Inquisition (*102*) was no worse than that of lay authorities; torture was not often used, for the threat of it, together with the threat of imprisonment of unknown duration, loosened most tongues. And when

102　The Inquisition

all due processes had been accomplished the accused, if penitent, was received back into the bosom of the Church. The trial was secret but the profession of penitence and acceptance, known as an *auto-da-fé* or act of faith, was public. The *auto-da-fé* formed a species of public entertainment not infrequently connected with some day of royal or civic rejoicing, the theory being that the crowds were assembled to witness the saving of a sinner. The condemned, both penitent and impenitent, wore the *sanbenito*, a loose garment marked with certain symbols (*103*). The *sanbenito* of the penitent

103   Execution after an *auto-da-fé*: the victim wears the *sanbenito* of the condemned

bore a plain St Andrew's cross on back and front; for the impenitent the imagination of the designers ran riot, depicting devils and scenes of hell as a foretaste of the condemned's destination.

The procession of priests, soldiers, city officials and condemned having arrived at the public place, the ceremony usually commenced with a corporate profession of faith. A Spanish correspondent of the Fuggers reported one such *auto-da-fé* which took place in Seville on the Sunday of 3 May 1579. There were thirty-eight accused, whose crimes ranged from the trivial to the grave, and their punishments were accordingly graded. Luis Moreno, a baptised Moor who tried to escape to Barbary, presumably to rejoin his own people, 'was to be punished with the habit [the *sanbenito*] and four years' imprisonment. There he is to be instructed in the tenets of the Faith, and receive 100 strokes of the

104   Methods of execution
Sixteenth-century woodcut from Nuremberg

rod.' A negro slave received two years imprisonment for denying the miracles of Christ; a blasphemer had his tongue pinioned; others were scourged or condemned to the galleys. The terrible punishment of death at the stake was reserved only for those totally impenitent of the graver crimes, and on this May Sunday the crowd were entertained by the sight of only one human being expiring in agony. He was one 'Orbian, native of Flanders, a binder by trade in his thirtieth year. He had burnt different paintings with the picture of Our Lord Jesus Christ thereon and put his faith entirely in the teachings of Luther.' He could have obtained the mercy of being strangled before the fire was lit had he confessed at the very last, but this he declined. The punishment of these thirty-eight must have occupied a large part of that Sunday, and it was with a heartfelt 'Vale! I rejoice that this is at an end' that the correspondent ended his letter.

Chapter VII

THE WORLD OF LEARNING

PRINTING

THE art of printing came full formed into the world at the precise moment that it was needed. Printing was a result, not a cause, of the intellectual ferment at work within Europe but without it that ferment would have been limited, for men would have been forced to continue to work in small, isolated groups. Before the invention, every book in the world was a handwritten work. There was an army of copiers in each centre of learning, at each great court, and a book deemed valuable could be assured of reproduction into hundreds of copies. But such reproduction was done without overall plan; a scholar desiring a work would have to locate a copy, commission a copier and pay him for the scores of hours the task would occupy. The chance of error through ignorance or negligence on the part of the copiers would multiply with each successive edition of a work, so that eventually the establishing of a correct text became a major problem. The great works of history, such as the Bible, were ensured a continued existence for there was always someone, somewhere, who desired his own copy. But the works of unknown men were limited to the few copies circulated among friends, and, if immediate interest ceased, then the book would disappear for years or perhaps for ever. As a result, men again and again tackled problems which had been solved by others in distant places and times. Printing opened a channel of communication of a kind which had never before been seen. The work of the few was swiftly available to the many, and among the many were those who could take the work a stage further and, in their turn, publish the results to an even wider audience.

The controversy regarding the true inventor of printing is very nearly as old as the art itself. In 1499 the Chronicler of Cologne firmly stated that it was the work of 'a burgher of Mainz, born at Strasburg, called Junker Johan Gutenberg'. The Chronicler was bitterly attacked by those anxious to claim the honour for their own country, but all available evidence substantiates him. Gutenberg was born sometime between 1394 and 1399. Typically, most of what is known of him is gleaned from a series of law suits which he seems to have conducted with an aggressive verve. In 1439 he was brought to court by the brothers of a man who had been his partner but who had died before the object of their partnership was achieved. The brothers sought to obtain details of a 'secret process' which the partners had been working upon; their law suit failed, but from it arose the first indications of printing in Europe.

The details of the case were necessarily kept vague; there was no patent law to protect a new invention and it suited all concerned to keep the facts to themselves. But the disputed process almost certainly related to the making of a type-mould. There was further talk of a 'press' which had been in the dead man's possession, but that was a common object. Variants of a screw with a handle which, when pulled down, would exert great pressure upon a plate were already in wide use. Gutenberg's unique contribution to the great inventions of the world was not printing, as such, but the means of producing thousands of movable letters all exactly alike. Printing —the transferring of marks from a raised surface to a flat one— was already very old. Gutenberg must have been familiar with the crude playing-cards of his day, produced from woodcuts to which coloured inks were applied and printed on paper. There was even a method to print the titles of books upon the covers by means of large letters carved in brass, and during Gutenberg's lifetime the principle of carving a whole page of text upon a single block of wood was introduced into Europe. These block-books enjoyed wide popularity but their use was limited to the reproduction of short, popular texts for which there was a steady demand. It required many hours' work to produce a single block which could be used only for the specific book for which it was carved. Mass-production of lengthy works required one vital component: movable letters which could be swiftly arranged in the innumerable combinations which make up words.

The scant evidences of Gutenberg's early life show that, at various periods he was associated with the manufacture of small, metal objects. Mainz was well known for the precision of its workers in precious metals, and Gutenberg's own family long had connections with the Archbishop's mint. He was therefore familiar with the problems of casting and stamping metal to a high degree of precision. This was to be the key to the problem. Wooden letters

162

each had to be carved by hand and the most skilled woodcarver would introduce variants in each, which accumulated as they were placed together. Metal can be melted and poured into a mould, thus providing a swift and simple method of producing thousands of identical shapes; the material can also be used again when the shape is blurred. Gutenberg's invention brought together two familiar objects; a punch and a mould. The punch was in hard metal and on its head was carved the letter or symbol required. On being struck into a piece of soft metal — the matrix — the

105   Printing press of 1507
From a contemporary woodcut

punch would transfer an exact impression of the letter or symbol. The matrix was then inserted into the base of a rectangular mould of the size required, hinged to allow extraction of the finished type, and molten metal poured in. The principle was simple but its application was costly. Gutenberg had to bear all the heavy costs of an ordinary printer, and at the same time have reserves in hand to meet the scores of problems which any new process encounters. He succeeded in perfecting his invention but he lacked business ability; even as he entered history through a law suit, so he left, being sued by Johan Fust, a goldsmith who had put up capital for a certain major production. Gutenberg was unable to pay and his entire equipment passed into the hands of another man.

Printing was an accepted fact by at least 1460. Two years after this date civil war broke out in Mainz and the little group of printers established there were forced to leave, and settled throughout Europe. In 1465 printing had reached Italy; five years later a press was established in France. The Low Countries followed and there, in the city of Bruges, an Englishman named William Caxton learned the new art and later founded his own press 'at the sign of the Red Pale', near Westminster Abbey in London.

The rapid growth of printing depended upon the supply of a cheap and abundant material to print upon. Parchment and vellum had been used in the learned world for hundreds of years, but they were so expensive as writing materials that it was a common habit to scrape a manuscript clean and use the material again for a new work. A cheap, durable and easily produced material was required to match the mass-production capabilities of the printing press, and the printers found it in paper. It had first been introduced into Europe during the twelfth century in response to the demand arising from the growth of universities; printing boosted that demand, making large-scale paper-manufacture an economic proposition. The common ingredient was linen rags, boiled to a pulp and beaten to a creamy consistency. A shallow wooden frame, with a bottom of closely woven wires, was dipped into the pulp and, when lifted out, surplus water would drain away, leaving a thick residue in the tray. The workman would give the tray a shake to cause the fibres to interlock, and the page of wet paper would be dumped out to dry (106). It later became common to weave some device into the wire bottom which would imprint itself upon the pulp, thereby forming a watermark. This simple method produced an attractive material so durable that books made from it exist today, 500 years later, with little or no deterioration. Paper was supplied to the printer in pages and not in rolls, each sheet being precisely the size of the tray in which it was made.

The vital typecasting section of a printing works had the simplest of equipment; a furnace, bellows, ladle and a supply of the precious moulds (107). The cutting of the punches and the preparation of the matrixes would already have been done by a skilled

106 The paper-maker

man, probably a goldsmith by training. The typecasters' work was largely mechanical. A minute quantity of the molten metal was poured into the mould; it would set almost immediately and a twist of the fingers released the gleaming new type. Examined for imperfections, the rough edges would be filed off and it would join the rest in a basket. The letters would be sorted and passed on to the compositor. The earliest known illustration of a printing press occurs in a Danse Macabre of 1499, where Death is shown come to drag the workmen away to his Dance (*108*). All the essential details are clearly vis-

107   Casting type
Woodcut from a 'Book of Trades'

ible; the compositor with his case of type, the unwieldly press itself where Death has seized the pressman just as he is about to pull the great lever, and a workman wielding the inkballs with which the type was inked. A page of manuscript is propped up before the compositor and he is in the act of picking up type. These will be slipped into the composing stick in his left hand and then transferred to the two-page forme beside him on the bench. In its turn, the full forme was transferred to a stone bed on the press itself, where it was inked. The sheet of paper to be printed was placed upon a hinged container and an outer leaf—the tympanum—brought down upon it. The tympanum was covered with a sheet of vellum with an area cut in the centre precisely the size of the type area. This was to protect the margins of the sheet from any dirt or ink which might lay upon the surrounding equipment which held the type. As soon as the sheet was in position, type and paper were slid under the plate of the press, the screw tightened and the plate brought into contact with the paper, exerting a heavy but smooth pressure.

In spite of the slowness of this work the most ambitious projects

108 Death and the printers
From a French 'Danse Macabre', 1499

were successfully undertaken. The earliest pieces of printed work were indulgences —simple, one-sheet productions, but very shortly afterwards work began on a book which, even today, would rank as a major publishing project. This was the great '42-line Bible'—so called from the numbers of lines on each page—which was probably begun by Gutenberg in partnership with Fust. Judged by any standard, this first of the world's printed books remains one of the most beautiful. The object of the first typefounders was exactly to copy the existing fashion in manuscript writing, and so successful were they that it takes a trained eye to detect a difference between a manuscript and an early printed book. It long remained the custom to add illuminated initials and rubrics by hand. The new craft did not at once cause the collapse of the copying industry; wealthy scholars were at first prejudiced against the use of print, deeming it an unworthy method to enshrine the thoughts of the great. But increasingly, scribes and copiers found themselves employed only for special, luxurious works. The demand for cheap, duplicated books grew with the supply, for Europe was hungry for learning.

SCIENCE

It was not until the eighteenth century that the term 'science' became restricted to the meaning that it bears today, and another century passed before the 'scientist' appeared as a special kind of scholar. Throughout the Renaissance 'science' was used in its original broad sense of 'knowledge'. In their passion for all things Greek, scholars made no distinction between scientific or humanist works; both were studied avidly, their corrupt texts corrected and added to the body of knowledge. Nevertheless, as the long-lost hoard of Greek knowledge was gradually restored to circulation, there inevitably developed specialisation. There were some, such as Leonardo da Vinci, who ranged freely over the entire spectrum of the physical world in an apparently inexhaustible curiosity; some again attempted to make a synthesis, to restore to a rapidly fragmenting universe that unity which had belonged to it in Greek philosophy. Giordano Bruno believed that he had succeeded, declared that God and His creation were one and the same thing, and was burnt for it—a new kind of martyr marking a new kind of heresy. But most recognised their limitations and pursued only segments of the vast field opening before them. Unlike its sister studies, physical science developed only sporadically during the fifteenth and sixteenth centuries, but those areas in which it surged forward immediately touched the common man: for they were concerned with the plants at his feet, the stars above him and his own body.

The total acceptance of the classic authors, the assumption that they had spoken once and for all time, later produced a strong reaction against them as their limitations were discovered. A French scholar of the sixteenth century, indeed, defended with some success the thesis that Aristotle, the doyen of scientists and philosophers, had been wrong throughout. The clearest example of this process occurred in botany. The writings of Pliny and Aristotle on the subject were naturally concerned with the flora of their own, southern, area. Northern observers, comparing text-book descriptions with an actual, northern, specimen before them, obviously found discrepancies. The discovery established a valuable precedent: it was dangerous to follow blindly even the most revered author—personal experiment alone could correct an apparent error. Men therefore left the study and the comparison of texts, and went out into the field. The country hitherto had been viewed as a strategic area to be fought for, or a machine for producing food; the civilised man lived in large communities behind strong walls, passing through the dangerous open country with the greatest speed. Poets and writers who sang the beauties of natural scenery had been very few and far between. Now there dawned a delight in Nature for her own sake so that, by 1542, a German could write: 'There is no one who does not know that there is nothing in this world pleasanter and more delightful than to wander over woods and mountains garlanded and adorned with little flowers, gazing intently upon them.'

Botany served a practical and immediate purpose, placing in the hands of the physician an increasing number of medicinal herbs. The first botanical garden was established in Padua in 1542 and the *herbarium*, the collection of dried plants, appeared not long afterwards. No technical language existed to describe specimens adequately, and botanists were forced to rely upon illustrators. These tended at first to copy the actual specimen before them, faithfully recording every individual defect, but there evolved a class of illustrator who was capable of going beyond the individual and illustrating the species. The *Herbals* or *Gardens of Health*, which appeared in abundance during the sixteenth century, were intended primarily as textbooks, but the high level of illustration and printing employed produced a book beautiful in its own right. Zoology, proceeding in much the same way, was less well served than botany for its practical application was of less value. Never-

theless, the growing ability of scholars to co-operate produced a number of major works during the sixteenth century, which included not only single books but encyclopaedias. The Swiss, Conrad Gesner, took 36 years to produce his *History of Animals*—an impressive example of scholastic and financial co-operation. He attempted a very rough classification and his descriptions of known land animals was generally accurate. Sea creatures presented a certain problem. As the frontiers of the known world were extended, so the places where monsters, beloved of the popular mind, could exist became less. The depths of the sea were, and long remained, the last outpost of the mysterious; even to-day, perennial news of the sea-serpent or

109 Gesner's bishop fish

the Loch Ness Monster can cause a stir. No one could contradict the author who peopled the deep waters with the most bizarre creatures, and Gesner faithfully produced some of them, though declining to comment on the reality of their existence (*109*).

ASTRONOMY

Renaissance science tended to the speculative rather than the experimental, so that the greatest discovery arose out of pure mathematics. The use of Arabic numbers became common, together with the now conventional mathematical symbols of plus, minus, etc. In 1584 a treatise on decimals appeared and sometime towards the end of the sixteenth century John Napier perfected the system of logarithms which enormously speeded calculations. But all these were tools, individually important, but even in their sum they appear trivial compared with that discovery made, without their aid, in the field of astronomy. This was a subject in which the most ignorant, the most humble, felt capable of expressing an opinion—for did not the same sky cover all, were not the stars and planets visible to shepherd and scholar alike? More ominously for its practitioners, it was a subject which touched the dangerous field of religion. It was, however, a canon of the Church, Nicolas Copernicus, who first tentatively opened a window on to the Universe. He was born in 1473, the son of a Polish merchant, and successfully combined a career as scholar and church official. His research was conducted more in the study than in the observatory, for it was by comparing the existing astronomical theories that he devised his own, which eliminated many of the contradictions.

There were two major, conflicting schools: that of Aristotle and Ptolemy, held by the Church and the universities, which saw the earth as the fixed centre of the universe, and that of Pythagoras, which maintained that earth with her sisters travelled around the sun. For over thirty years Copernicus pondered the problem, circulating his theory in manuscript among fellow scholars. It was not for fear of religious persecution that he long delayed publication but from the far more common fear of ridicule, for his theory was so obviously at variance with both observable phenomena and accepted ideas. He maintained the theory of crystalline spheres which carried the heavenly bodies, revolving inside each other, but insisted that, mathematically, the earth must revolve on its own axis and move around the sun. The system involved concepts which could not be demonstrated with the primitive instruments then available. The phenomenon of parallax, for example, in which a fixed star will appear to move as a result of the earth's own movement around the sun, was not observed until the nineteenth century. But, to both hostile scholars and the ordinary man, the most ludicrous aspect of the new theory was its attribution of motion to the earth when every sense showed that it stood still. In vain Copernicus argued from classical literature: 'It is the same thing as Aeneas says in Virgil, "We sail forth from the harbour and lands and cities retire".' Common sense was on the side of his attackers. If the earth moved, then birds and missiles would be left behind, a falling stone would never reach the ground, the very air would be whisked off the globe. It was manifest nonsense. Copernicus had good cause to keep his theories private for as long as possible, even though he was encouraged by the Vatican in its desire to establish a reform of the calendar. Tradition has it that the first printed copy of *On the Revolution of Celestial Orbs* was placed in his hands on the very day of his death in 1543.

Copernicus was attacked as heartily by scholars as by poets. Even the first true astronomer, the Danish Tycho Brahe (*110*), totally rejected the heliocentric theory. Unlike Copernicus, Brahe based his researches upon direct observation and established Europe's first effective observatory. It was from there that he observed the series of comets which followed the appearance of a nova in the constellation of Cassiopeia. Comets could find no place in

110   Tycho Brahe in his observatory

the rigid Copernician system of crystalline spheres, and Brahe therefore eliminated them all save for one great sphere which held the firmament. But Brahe's main contribution was less the construction of new theories than the compilation of an enormous mass of data which, in time, were employed by his assistant, Johann Kepler, in the construction of his laws of planetary motion.

Astronomers were working virtually blindfolded until 1609, when the Italian Galileo Galilei learned that 'a certain Fleming had constructed a spyglass by means of which visible objects, though very distant from the eyes of the observer, were distinctly seen as though nearby'. A year later Galileo perfected his own instrument which magnified 1,000 times, and brought an object apparently thirty times closer. He called it an *occhiale*, or spyglass, but in 1611 the word 'telescope' was coined for the instrument which allowed an observer to stand above the earth and gain the first true picture of the Universe. Much of Galileo's observation confirmed the theory of Copernicus, establishing finally that the earth was only one, and that among the least, of a family attendant upon the sun enthroned in the centre. It sparked off, too, the bitter quarrel between science and religion which marked the seventeenth and following centuries.

ANATOMY

One of the more common objects of the period was the human corpse. Plague and war would provide hundreds or thousands within a short time; the gibbet outside every city would display the decomposing bodies of criminals; periodic persecutions of Jews, witches or heretics would provide yet more. Most were buried, but some were not, either as punishment or from neglect in the sparsely populated countryside. Vesalius, the anatomist, could relate quite casually: 'While out walking, looking for bones on the country highways, where those who have been executed are commonly placed, I happened upon a dried cadaver'. The corpse or its skeleton appeared again and again in representations of Death as a person. Yet, in spite of this familiarity, man knew almost as little about the structure of his own body as he did about the structure of the solar system. It was the classic example of looking without seeing, of relying without question upon the work of an established authority. The authority in medicine and anatomy was Galen, a Greek physician who died in A.D. 199; his own experiments in dissection were limited to animals, and the obvious differences between his descriptions and observed fact were explained by the argument that the body of man had changed during the intervening centuries. Galen described the human thighbone as curved; Renaissance thighbones had therefore been made straight by the tight, narrow trousers of the day.

In 1543 there appeared a work *On the Structure of the Human Body*, which both established the ground for modern medicine and anatomy and made a landmark in printing. Its author, Andreas Vesalius, was descended from three generations of physicians and from boyhood was versed in dissection (*111*). Coming at length to study Galen, he was astonished by the errors which others had been content to accept, and, with a confidence amounting to arrogance, set about to correct the master. His own work appeared when he was only twenty-seven; it was a superb production, illustrated with 277 woodcuts of a quality which can only be called art. It was rumoured indeed that some were produced in the studio of Titian himself. They performed their function of anatomical description but the artists had included with each illustration some delightful,

111   Vesalius conducting a public dissection
Detail from the title-page of his 'De humani corporis fabrica'

irrelevant detail in the background, humanising the whole. The frontispiece itself has become one of the most famous pictures, showing Vesalius, a dark, handsome young man, lecturing a group of students, his face turned to the reader, his left hand firmly supporting a half-dissected human arm (*112*). Vesalius made errors of commission and omission; he showed the true course of veins and the structure of the heart, but did not comprehend the circulation of the blood. But he had made the great crossing from ancient to modern anatomy, providing a guide for a new generation of surgeons to follow.

112   Andreas Vesalius
The frontispiece of his famous work

THE ALCHEMISTS

At about the same time that Copernicus and his fellows were evolving an ordered scheme for the physical world, there grew to a peak an art or science which was half quackery, half wisdom, a study rooted in mysticism but dealing with the real bones of the earth. In the eighteenth century, when alchemy was at last dying, a Frenchman looked back over its 3,000-year history and summed it up as 'the history of the greatest folly and the greatest wisdom of which man is capable'.

Alchemic processes were obscure, partly from the complexity of their nature, partly from the desire of the practitioners to hide from common persons the secrets of the Great Art. The alchemist was not merely a worker in metals and chemicals but a philosopher and a mystic, searching all aspects of creation for the ultimate key. His art was founded by the god Hermes, whence the terms Hermetic Art and the Sons of Hermes were used allusively for alchemy and alchemists. It had been practised in ancient Egypt and China, but European alchemists derived their laws from the so-called Emerald Tablet of Laws found in a cave with the dead body of Hermes some aeons after the Flood.

The central core of alchemy was the search for the Philosopher's Stone (*113*). To the commercially-minded the Stone was merely that which, when brought into contact with a base metal, would turn it to gold 10, 100 or 1,000 times multiplied. But to the true alchemist the Stone was much more. Gold was not desired for its own sake but because it was deemed to be the most perfect of metals; it was held that all metals would be gold if they could but were prevented by the impurities of the earth. The Stone was believed to be a pure matter, perfect in itself, which would transform all imperfections.

113 Emblems of the Philosopher's Stone

It became the Elixir of Life which would prolong human life, restore youth and health; it would enable man to understand the language of the beasts, spy out distant lands, reform evil characters, improve agriculture. Most important of all, it did not come from Satanic sources but, being distilled from the resources of God's own creation, could not be anything but wholesome. Its description and names are as innumerable as the hopes entertained for it: Brass of Philosophers, Virgin's Milk, Shadow of the Sun, Dry Water, Serpent's Brother, Grand Magisterium—one list alone gives 600 names for it. Preliminaries for its preparation were known as the Minor Work, the preparation itself as the Great Work. Descriptions of the process abound but so couched in symbolism and ritual are they that it is probable that only another alchemist could understand them. Essentially, ordinary gold, silver, sulphur and mercury were purified again and again in the Vase of Hermes, an hermetically-sealed glass vessel shaped like an egg. The resulting 'philosopher's gold, sulphur, or silver' would again be distilled with

114 The First Key of Basil Valentine

every conceivable ingredient which would undergo a chemical change with heat.

Much of the body of alchemic law is in the form of illustrations, which, with their juxtaposition of incongruous objects, curiously resemble the Surrealism of the twentieth century. Most of the illustrations were statements of chemical processes, the elaborate allegory taking the place of modern chemical formulae. Thus the four degrees of heat, required at different stages of the Great Work, were represented by four seated women each crowned with the sun, representing the sun's heat in four signs of the Zodiac. The famous 12 Keys of Basil Valentine sum up in one fascinating series all that was mystical, allegorical, but also practical in alchemy. The name 'Basil Valentine' was itself a characteristic allegory and was probably the pseudonym of a monk living in the late fifteenth century. The Keys were considered to be his last will and testament, and provided instruction, from the first to the final process, to those who had already passed the preliminary stages. The first Key shows the essential purification of gold (*114*). The king represents the metal, the queen is silver, the wolf is antimony (a corrosive) and the old man represents fire. The king is to be fed to the wolf, which is then to be burnt, 'and by this process the king will be liberated and rendered fit for the first stage of our work'. The last Key is the most potent. 'He that possesses the tincture and is unacquainted with its use might as well not have it at all. Therefore this twelfth and last Key must open up to you the uses of this stone.' Here the lion is the Stone itself devouring the serpent (base metal), which will be transformed into its own flesh. There were many emblems for the actual Stone, one of which shows it as a cube flanked by seven flowers for the seven planets and their associated metals. Above it is the sign for the metal mercury flanked by the moon (silver) and the sun (gold). Above that again is the sign for sulphur surrounding the phoenix and dominating all the crowned king, flanked by fire and the blood of the pelican, the pelican being a form of retort or alembic(*113*).

In its last stages, alchemy came to be dominated by charlatans supposedly capable of making gold from any base metal, actually highly practised in parting fools from their money. In 1589 the hard-headed citizens of Venice accorded a certain Bragadini, one of these 'alchemists', a reverence they denied ordinary monarchs. 'Such a host of princes and lords beleagured him that he was hardly safe although he has a bodyguard of fifty archers. He literally throws gold about by the shovelful.' Firm report came that Bragadini had presented the city with two ampullas of a liquid which turned quicksilver into gold to the tune of six million ducats. 'I doubt not but that this will appear mighty strange but must be believed for every-

115   Alchemists at work

176

thing is so open that it cannot be doubted.' A month after this report and Bragadini had still not been unmasked. 'The night before last he made two ingots, each one of the weight of one pound, in the presence of some of our patrician aldermen. There no longer exists any doubt upon the matter.'

Bragadini was only one of a tribe of conjurors who did indeed make gold, if not for their employers. The use that Ben Jonson makes of the jargon of the trade in *The Alchemist* illustrates how widespread was the trickery; even an illiterate audience knew enough to understand allusions to griffins' eggs, the crow's return, earth's fatness and the scores of other colourful terms. Many of the tricksters found themselves in dungeons, or were burnt alive by irate dupes calling upon the Holy Office to punish them, not as alchemists, but as magicians. But others became wealthy. They were perforce nomads, hastily moving on before their victims discovered that the expensively obtained 'Philosopher's Stone' was worth no more than the material of which it was made. These were the men who brought alchemy to an inglorious close, but in its heyday it performed a great service to the cause of science. In the search for the Stone every possible substance was examined and subjected to chemical processes, and from these experiments arose a wide knowledge of mineralogy and chemistry. Ironically, it was not the pure, philosophical alchemist who laid the foundations of modern chemistry but the despised Puffer, the man who hunted gold for commercial reasons. And though the Philosopher's Stone eluded pure and impure alchemist alike, yet from the fires of countless furnaces was precipitated, by accident, the Devil's Stone known as gunpowder.

EDUCATION

The common idea that, the clergy apart, a total illiteracy prevailed throughout the Middle Ages is one which dies hard but has little basis in fact. A great number of ordinary people, during the course of their everyday work, had to have some knowledge of book-learning. Seamen, merchants, agents of landlords—all those whose work required the regular compilation or consultation of lists must have known their alphabet and possessed the rudiments of mathematics. Education, however, was in general regarded with justifiable suspicion by all forms of authority; if it was impossible to suppress, it was advisable to control. Richard II of England displayed considerable enlightenment when, in 1391, he not merely rejected the petition of certain landowners who sought to prevent their serfs' children from attending school, but decreed that any parent in his kingdom was free to send his child to school—if a school could be found. The great rent which the Reformation made in the fabric of Europe, a little over a century later, destroyed much of the existing system of education. Luther, in his forthright and prejudiced manner, summed up that old system as one which provided 'only enough bad Latin [to enable a man] to become a priest ... and yet remain all his life a poor ignoramus, fit neither to cackle nor lay eggs'. Luther had an axe to grind, but the more temperate Erasmus echoed him, writing with contempt of his own childhood education as a memorising of foolish Latin verse among coarse, illiterate men. He was as disenchanted with the University of Paris. 'I carried away nothing but a body infected with disease and a plentiful supply of vermin.'

But there was little basic change in the practice during the sixteenth century (117). Schools in Protestant countries were secularised, though the curriculum still gave pride of place to religious and classic studies. An English traveller in Germany in 1600 believed that all Germans, even the lowest classes, had at least a passing acquaintance with Latin, arithmetic and music. In England, over 200 new schools came into existence during the latter half of the sixteenth century, supplying the place of those monastic schools which had been swept away. In response to the Protestant challenge, the great order of the Jesuits was formed in 1540, one of their declared aims being 'the education of children and other persons ignorant in Christianity'. In their abandonment of the idea that the rod was the only means of forcing information into the heads of the reluctant, the Jesuits made a considerable step forward in pedagogical theory. They sought rather to spur their pupils forward by mutual rivalry, dividing classes under some such names as Rome and Carthage and pitting the two sections against each other. But the Jesuit aim was a child skilled in receiving ideas rather than in speculating about them, able to dazzle in debate rather than initiate original work.

It was long before the more liberal theories of education found their way into practice. There was a growing awareness that education should have a broader base, infused with the humanities and producing at length 'a wise and eloquent piety'. In England

Sir Thomas Elyot's *Boke Named the Governour* outlined the education of a gentleman as being balanced both physically and mentally, games and sports of equal value with formal learning. Football as a sport, however, was to be avoided, 'for therein is nothing but beastly fury and external violence'. In Paris, a Spaniard levelled an attack upon the current method of university education by means of debate, a method which exalted sophistry at the expense of truth. Even Erasmus, most unlikely of pedagogues, gave to the world a theory which, though vague in detail was excellent in outline. 'I have no patience

116 Flogging *From a Florentine spelling primer, c. 1500*

with the average teacher of grammar who wastes precious years hammering rules into children's heads.' Language should be mastered casually, by talking and reading and children could be taught 'without the customary flogging', a casual remark which gives a clear idea of the current teaching practices (*116*). But there was little in teaching to attract an able man: hours were long, salary was poor, discipline required a thick skin and a strong arm, and the profession had little social status.

The three levels of education were elementary, grammar and university. Before the Reformation the monastic school predominated, although there were also schools endowed by charity or supported by the guilds. It was long before the printing press supplied schools with even a minimum of the necessary textbooks and, at the elementary level, the horn book which had been for many years the symbol of the young student was still much in evidence. It was a piece of parchment, backed by a stout board and

117   An Elizabethan school

protected by a thin layer of transparent horn upon which the Lord's Prayer, the alphabet and one or two basic rules of grammar were written. Once the student had passed this very elementary stage, the horn book would be handed on to a younger brother. Religious instruction learned parrot fashion, reading, writing, arithmetic and singing, these were the basic elements of the elementary school. The '*grammatica*' taught at the grammar schools was very wide, including not only grammar and composition in the student's native language but also classic Latin and literature. A boy's parents would receive regular indication of his progress in the language for his letters home would be written in Latin. The need to translate requests for clothes, money and food into a dead language must have reduced many a small boy to tears. At university, an undergraduate's progress was very similar to the progress of an apprentice in any other craft (*118*). His course lasted seven years; halfway through he became a *baccalaureus*, the equivalent of a journeyman in a craft, and, on becoming a master at the end, he gave a lecture as his masterpiece.

The education of women lagged far behind, but was not ignored. Daughters of the aristocracy were taught at home, some of their tutors being among the foremost scholars. Merchants' daughters found a schooling in nunneries not much worse than their brothers found in monastic or guild schools. No one troubled about the daughters of the poor: to be able to spin, sew, cook, and in general manage a house was considered sufficient education. It was a hard, but necessary custom. The greater part of those household necessities which are today provided for money, were made by the woman of the house.

The life of a student was hard. At Eton in 1530, the day began at 6 a.m.; a quarter of an hour was allowed for breakfast at 9 a.m.; there was a break at 11 a.m. for dinner and the scholars supped at 5 p.m. and were in bed shortly afterwards. At Cambridge

> there be divers which rise daily about four or five of the clock in the morning and from five till six of the clock use common prayer with an exhortation of God's word in a common chapel and from six till ten of the clock use ever either private study or common lectures. At ten of the clock they go to dinner (where one pennyworth of beef serves for four). After this slender diet they be either teaching or learning until five of the clock in the evening, when they sup not much better than their dinner. Immediately after which they go either to reasoning in problems or to some other study until it be nine or ten of the clock; and then being without fires, are fain to walk or run up and down half an hour to get a heat on their feet when they go to bed.

A day beginning at 5 a.m., and continuing until 9 or 10 p.m., merely reflected the working hours of common people. The son of the great carried his normal style of life into the university. It was accepted that his academic superiors would remember their station in life as his social inferior and that he himself would be exempt from the punishments inflicted upon his fellows. The lot of the poor student was quite different. Usually he was earning his keep, sometimes by honest labour, sometimes by begging, sometimes by banditry. The food he ate was vile; the already slender sum alloted for his victuals would be whittled down by dishonest servants, and rotten meat, mouldy bread and sour wine were his normal fare. His recreations inside the university were limited to the point of non-existence. The common sports of dicing, cockfighting, bearbaiting were, naturally enough, forbidden but so were the harmless

118 Master and students at a university

pleasures of dancing, dining or ordinary games. His major recreation was in the town-versus-gown riots, which were a feature of every city in which a university was established. The townsfolk had little time for the students; they brought no money and filled the city with their disturbances. On the other hand, students found themselves cheated as a matter of course. The mutual dislike frequently spilled over into open warfare. In Erfurt, students murdered an innkeeper who dared to ask for his bill. The citizens, unable to obtain satisfaction from the university authorities, actually dragged up a cannon and bombarded the university dormitory. The great school of the Sorbonne in the University of Paris was a permanent centre of riot. Youths who had begged, fought and robbed their way across Europe to attend the university were not inclined to be particularly gentle in their treatment of Parisians. Some of them actually formed armed bands and terrorised the city and outskirts until they were suppressed by savage retaliation from the city authorities. A university man was well equipped for the battle of life by the time he had obtained his degree.

Chapter VIII

THE CITY OF GOD

RELIGION was woven into the very fabric of society, as much a part of it as the use of gold in commerce, of force in war. Its physical manifestations were everywhere visible, for the smallest village had its church, the most arrogant city its cathedral and entire communities existed only because of a nearby monastery or centre of pilgrimage. There was hardly a family who could not claim a priest as relative. On the highways the friar was as common a traveller as the soldier or merchant; in the cities the brown, black, grey, or white uniforms of religion wove a sober thread through the multi-coloured throngs in the streets. The very expletives that men used—'Swounds' (God's wounds), 'oddsbody' (God's body—the Host), 'gadzooks' (God's hooks—the nails of the Cross)—were sacrilegious, but rendered colourless by usage; a period of time might be measured by the time taken to say a prayer; peasant and noble, merchant and craftsman alike engaged in religious controversy with a passion which in other times might be devoted to politics. Men died by the thousand in war or upon the scaffold, defending or attacking the precise interpretation of a theological point.

The church itself was the natural centre of the community (*119*). Until the latter half of the sixteenth century, when buildings devoted solely to the theatre began to appear, it was the only public place for indoor gatherings. Often it had been built by the voluntary labour of villagers or citizens and was supported by their alms. Their very familiarity with it made them unaware of, or indifferent to, the sacred quality of the building and they subjected it to indignities against which prelates thundered in vain. Daily attendance at Mass was a commonplace, and it was therefore natural that the church should become a casual meeting place. Banquets were held in the nave and in times of war the massive structure could provide a refuge or a storehouse. These usages accustomed the people to using it as a covered thoroughfare and worse. St

119   The church as a meeting place

Paul's in London became notorious as a 'house of talking, brawling, of minstrelsy, of hawks and of dogs'. Every great church witnessed the sacrilege of the money-lender pursuing his trade within sight of the high altar, the haggling of petty merchants in the naves or street women plying for hire, protected from inclement weather. The churchyard was both thoroughfare and marketplace; sometimes, as with St Paul's, the respectable profession of bookselling grew up within its shadow but, as often, the trades plied there were infamous. The deliberate desecration which marked the peak of puritan fanaticism was no worse than the casual desecration which was a commonplace long before the Reformation.

Pilgrims who still took the road were scarcely distinguishable from folk going about their ordinary business. Gone was the sober robe, the staff and wallet which proclaimed their status and protected them from all but the most resolute evil-doer. They wore the gay clothes of people on holiday, whiled away the journey with secular pleasures and, arriving at their destination, discharged their duty in a perfunctory manner which enraged the devout. The pilgrimage played more the part of the conducted tour of later centuries than the penitential journey of earlier. Like the later tourist, the pilgrim would bring home souvenirs, but these were of holy or supernatural origin. Feathers from the wing of the Archangel Gabriel; bones, of dubious origin, supposedly belonging to some saint; tears of the Madonna in a costly phial; fragments of the true Cross—all were for sale and found ready buyers. The peddlers were frequently holy friars, so-called, who made a fat living from the credulity of the ignorant. In Italy, particularly, these friars were responsible for much of the bitter anti-clericalism which existed alongside a deep and genuine devotion. 'They cheat and steal and when they are at the end of their resources, they set up as saints and work miracles, one displaying the cloak of St Vincent, another the handwriting of St Bernadino' or the bridle of another saint's horse. They staged elaborate deceptions, one of their number pretending to be blind, or lame, or suffering from leprosy, to be cured by the 'miraculous' touch of a confederate's cloak—parts of which could then be sold. Cloistered monks came under attack for their idle, luxury-loving lives.

> These well fed gentlemen with the capacious cowls do not pass their time in barefooted journeys and in sermons, but sit in elegant slippers, with their hands crossed over their paunches, in charming cells wainscotted with cyprus-wood. And when they are obliged to quit the house, they ride comfortably on mules and sleek, quiet horses. They do not overstrain their minds with the study of many books, for fear lest knowledge might put the pride of Lucifer in the place of monkish simplicity.

The bitterness of the accusations was an indication of the genuine devotion to the Christian Church which most men cherished; had they been indifferent to the institution they would have been indifferent to its custodians. They themselves might

120   Leo X in St Peter's

make a market-place of their parish church, drink and steal upon pilgrimages, but they expected something better from their spiritual leaders. That the guardians of the City of God should use their power to indulge worldly appetites was a source of shame to all who were aware of the nature of the thing that was being debased. For every debauched friar or cardinal there were hundreds of honourable clergy who pursued a demanding vocation to the best of their abilities. But it was the minority who attracted public atten-tion and whom the satirists pilloried for the wonder of posterity, and of that minority the worst found their home in the Papal court at the very heart of the organisation (*120*). The ferocious political battles in Rome, the scandals of nepotism, the moral degradation, left their indelible mark upon Christendom. The disillusionment of those scholars who had hoped to pursue a career in the service of the greatest institution of learning in the world found expression in snarling diatribes. One confessed that he would have followed Luther if he had been free, 'if only to see this swarm of scoundrels put back into their proper place, so that they may be forced to live either without vices or without power'. There were not lacking high prelates—cardinals, bishops and even popes—who attempted to cleanse the City but in the closed circle of power it was almost impossible to establish new principles. Reform, when it came, surged from below.

THE TWO MONKS

Attempts at local reform had occurred many times in different places in Europe over the past centuries. Some died a natural death, some were condemned as heresies, others still found their way into the main body of the Church, and, after the initial impetus, were thereby rendered respectable. The great movements were often without a head, for they were the spontaneous rising of the people, goaded beyond endurance by natural or man-made catastrophes, turning to God in final desperation. Those great processions of the Flagellants, which swept across Europe during the Black Death, were typical of this class. The vast numbers of people who took part made it impossible for authority to suppress the movement and the Church wisely went with the tide until it had receded. The Church could afford to do so, for such mass emotions had no aim and could be directed into a harmless channel. But now and again there arose a movement with a leader who could formulate the inarticulate hopes and fears of the led, threatening the existing structure both spiritual and temporal. Two such leaders arose within a generation of each other; both were monks, the one an Italian, Gioralamo Savonarola, the other a German, Martin Luther. The Italian achieved a brief period of absolute political and spiritual power within the

121   Savonarola preaching

city of Florence but died at length a felon's death. The German found himself, almost reluctantly, as the champion of half of Europe.

Savonarola came to power in Florence during one of the city's perennial disturbances (*121*). The Medici had been exiled, the citizens were at each others throats and the threat of the French invasion hung over all Italy. Men desperately needed a leader, a i. 'th-piece, and found it in the person of the Dominican monk who had already performed a tremendous task by cleansing his own monastery of San Marco of the abuses which seemed now to be an integral part of monastic life. He was prepossessing in neither appearance nor speech. The vivid portrait of him, painted by Fra Angelico whom he had converted, shows a forceful but ugly face with heavy lips, great beaked nose and burning eyes; contemporary reports of his sermons show that they were only average, both in content and delivery. But Italians were accustomed to great orators delivering impassioned sermons with a mechanical perfection; they stirred the listener while they were being delivered and then were forgotten. No man could doubt Savonarola's sincerity, the absolute conviction with which he warned of the wrath of God hovering over Italy. His prophecies and visions earned him a fame which went far beyond Florence. Lorenzo de' Medici clashed with him, was warned that within a year he would be dead—and died within that year. In distant Rome Alexander VI, the Borgia pope who embodied all the evils of a temporal papacy, marked down the intemperate monk for later attention as his attacks upon the corruption of the Papacy became ever more telling.

But for the moment Savonarola was secure among the tough citizens of Florence. He scourged them for their immorality and they flocked to his sermons by the thousand; he ordered them to cleanse their bodies and homes of the devil's frivolities and they burnt their precious ornaments in the main square. This too was an *auto-da-fé*—but objects, not men, were burnt. Scents, mirrors, false hair, musical instruments, carnival masks were piled high; books, too, were there, containing poems not only of the pagan poets but such respectable Christians as Petrarch. The great pile represented not only a cross-section of Renaissance art but a substantial cash value, and a Venetian merchant who happened to be present offered 22,000 florins for the objects. The Florentines replied by throwing his own portrait upon the pile before setting light to it. The reforming zeal became fanaticism; not the least unpleasant aspect was the bands of 'holy' children who roamed the city, seeking out further ornaments and fripperies of the devil. The Florentines abandoned their civic constitution for which they had shed so much blood over the centuries; Christ was proclaimed king of the city and Savonarola his vicar. The inevitable reaction set in; just a year after the triumphant *auto-da-fé* of 1497 his power crumbled. The people abandoned him to the powerful enemies who had been waiting this moment; he confessed that he had been deluded, his visions false, and he was first hanged, then burnt, in the same square where he believed that he had witnessed the triumph of Christ over the world (*94*).

Nineteen years after the ashes of Savonarola were thrown into the Arno, another Dominican monk was touring through Germany acting as a spiritual salesman. His name was Johann Tetzel and the wares he sold were slips of paper, bearing a printed promise of the remission of sins in return for gold (*122*). The pope at that time was Leo X, one of the most brilliant of Renaissance men: learned, cultured, affable, able to enjoy even the numerous satires directed against him. To him had fallen the enormous task of completing the new church of St Peter's which his predecessors had begun. Gold by the hundred thousand pieces was needed for the task and he sought it where he could. It happened that the bishop of Magdeburg in Germany desired to become archbishop of Mainz.

122 Sale of indulgences

Leo agreed, provided that he could raise the customary fees which, upon this occasion, were to be devoted to the building of St Peter's. The bishop in his turn borrowed money from the Fuggers and, in order to repay them—and with Leo's authority—set Tetzel the task of selling the indulgences. The Church's teaching upon this subject was highly complex but Tetzel reduced it to a simple formula: pay—and not only the souls of the dead would be pardoned but the buyer of an indulgence would be virtually free to commit what sins he liked.

> *As soon as the coin in the coffer rings*
> *The soul from purgatory springs.*

So a contemporary summed up Tetzel's cynical perversion of an article of faith. His progress through the German cities was like a triumph. Civic and ecclesiastic dignatories met him in each, accompanied him in solemn procession to some public place where he would set up his stand and launch into a money-charming speech. Beside him, keeping careful tally of the gold as it spilled into the chest, was a Fugger agent. He had much to do for Tetzel

123 Martin Luther
Engraving by Lucas Cranach, 1520

was overwhelmed by buyers and production of the little slips of paper in turn gave an impetus to the new-born art of printing. But among the many buyers were some who were offended by the gross sacrilege and it was through them that a copy of the indulgence came into the hands of Martin Luther with a request that he should comment upon it. On 31 October 1517 Luther nailed his ninety-five theses of comment upon the church door at Wittenberg.

Luther was then an Augustinian monk (*123*) and his act was by no means intended as a dramatic defiance of the pope; the church door customarily was used as a kind of bulletin board. Luther merely intended, and was understood to intend, that he was prepared to defend his theses in public debate against all comers. A year later he appeared before the papal legate at Augsburg where he defended his position. He still had neither desire nor intention of leading any kind of breakaway movement. In the April of that year he publicly acknowledged both the integrity of the pope and his own loyalty. 'Now at last we have a most excellent Pontiff, Leo X, whose integrity and learning are a delight to all men's ears. . . . Most blessed Father, I offer myself prostrate at the feet of your Holiness. I will acknowledge your voice as the voice of Christ, residing and speaking in you.' Leo, for his part, reacted with a commendable mildness, even issuing a bull in which the abuses of indulgences were condemned.

Luther's challenge to public debate was taken up by a certain John Eck at Leipzig and a contemporary, present at the debate, gives a description of the originator of the Reformation. 'Martin is of middle height, emaciated from care and study so that you can almost count the bones through his skin. He is in the vigour of manhood, and has a clear, penetrating voice. He is learned and has the Scriptures at his fingers' ends. A perfect forest of ideas and words stands at his command. He is affable and friendly and in no sense dour or arrogant. He is equal to anything.' There is no record of the result of the debate, but, during it, Luther finally committed himself and, in June 1520, Leo was forced to declare him a heretic and gave him sixty days to recant or be excommunicated. Neither side could withdraw. Leo was speaking in the name of an enormous and venerable organisation which, in its centuries of existence, had seen such rebels as Luther come and go by the hundred. Luther was claiming for untold thousands the right of acting according to individual conscience. It was an intellectual quarrel but each side was deeply enmeshed in national and political considerations, both pope and monk moved by forces which, though they could set in motion, they could not control. The drama of the Diet of Worms in April 1521, when the lone monk defended himself before the Emperor of Christendom and was formally condemned by him, had been centuries in preparation. The City of God was at last divided against itself.

The division first found expression in a bitter war of words. In no other field did the printing press have so enorm and immediate an effect, and as the struggle spread through the Continent so the stream of pamphlets and books became a flood. In Germany alone the number of books increased from 150 in 1518 to 990 in 1524. Violent language was well equalled by vicious caricatures, artists of every degree of ability turning their

124 Peasants plundering a monastery
After a sixteenth-century drawing

talents to the lampooning of religious enemies. It was not long before the war of words became the war of swords. The inarticulate mass of common people, particularly the peasants of Germany, had at last, they believed, found both a spokesman and an objective. As with all rebellions, the untutored ascribed all the evils of the human condition to the power being attacked. The price of bread, the arrogance of local officials, the monopolies of merchants—all these were now laid at the door of the papacy. If the power of the papacy were broken then Utopia would dawn, the arrogant would be thrust down and the humble exalted. So thought the peasants and banded together to break a slavery more grinding than serfs had ever known, convinced that Luther would lead them into that Utopia. Sympathetic at first, he yet feared, as all responsible men feared, the violence of men adrift in a new world which had not yet had time to form its own system of living. The peasants had objected to their condition of near-slavery. 'It has been the custom for men to hold us as their own property and this is pitiable, seeing that Christ redeemed and bought us with his blood. Therefore it agrees with Scripture that we be free.' Not so, replied Luther: even the prophets had slaves. 'Your article is against the Gospel . . . [for it] would make all men equal and that is impossible.' They condemned him as a traitor and swarmed across the country in an orgy of violence, wreaking upon the existing nobility the revenge that had been earned over centuries. Society, even if it called itself protestant or reformed, could not tolerate the threat to its very structure. Luther himself denounced the peasants' war, threw his weight upon the side of those who would destroy them. Inevitably the tide turned, for they were an undisciplined rabble, armed for the most part with the tools of their profession while opposing them were men bred to the art of warfare. Some 130,000 peasants died in Germany, baptising the Reformation in blood. They were but the first of many more throughout Europe as the rent in the fabric of Christendom spread from Germany.

Index

The numerals in **heavy type** refer to the figure numbers of the illustrations

INDEX

INDEX

If you would like to receive a newsletter
telling you about our new children's books,
fill in the coupon with your name and
address and send it to:

Gillian Osband, Transworld Publishers Ltd.,

57-59 Uxbridge Road, Ealing, London, W5

- - - - - - - - - - - - - - - -

Name ....

Address ....

....

....

CHILDRENS NEWSLETTER

HAVELOK THE WARRIOR *by Ian Serraillier*   20p

552 52007 1   Carousel Fiction

These are the days when evil men conspired to overthrow the monarchy, greedy for the power and wealth of wearing the crown and ruling the land. The King of Denmark is dead, his son Havelok forced to flee the murderous attempts of Earl Godard by escaping to the shores of England. He grows up to be a great warrior, to recover his kingdom.

THE BLACK PEARL *by Scott O' Dell*   20p

552 52008 X   Carousel Fiction

The Black Pearl belonged to the old men, with legends and stories to tell to pass the time—or so Ramon Salazar had thought, until he came face to face with the devilfish and the struggle for the pearl began. But Ramon had more than the dangers of the sea to conquer. Others wanted the Great Pearl of Heaven, including the evil Pearler from Seville.

THE STORY OF MAUDE REED *by Norah Lofts*   25p

552 52010 1   Carousel Fiction

Her grandfather was only a wool merchant and his house was not considered suitable for a young girl of noble blood. Maude was now old enough to be taught the accomplishments of a lady; sewing, music and the art of graceful behaviour. But this was the Fifteenth Century, and her school was to be an old, dark castle.

BETSY *by Dorothy Canfield* 25p

552 52029 Carousel Fiction

Elizabeth Ann was an orphan. She lived with her Great-Aunt Harriet and Aunt Frances, who looked after her so carefully that she was quite unable to do anything for herself. But when she was nine, Aunt Harriet became ill and had to go away with Aunt Frances to a warmer climate. Elizabeth Ann was sent to stay on her uncle's farm in Vermont. Poor Elizabeth Ann! There was no one to fuss over her now.

Her new family called her 'Betsy'. They never stopped to wonder whether anything was too hard for her to tackle—and Betsy began to discover how exciting it was to think for herself, to help on the farm, and to get herself out of difficult scrapes.

THE STORY OF BRITAIN *by R. J. Unstead* 30p

Series Carousel Non-Fiction

A country is forged by its history, the battles and intrigues of by-gone ages laying the foundations of today. From its beginnings as an island to the end of the Second World War, this series is the record of the men and women who played a role in shaping the character of England now. It traces the emergence of England as a nation.

LOOKING AND FINDING *by Geoffrey Grigson* 25p

552 54007 2 Carousel Non-Fiction

You can find sunken treasure, hidden away in some long-forgotten shipwreck, or discover the past through scattered fossils and ancient inscriptions. It depends what you're looking for, how you go about finding it. It depends where you're looking, how you go about getting there. But once the search begins, there's no knowing what you might stumble across.

TRUE MYSTERIES *by Robert Hoare*   25p

552 54009 9   Carousel Non-Fiction

Tales of the unknown, stories of people who suddenly appear and disappear without explanation, and strange events which present no logical answer, sometimes turning legend into fact, or fact into legend. And always leaving a question mark.

ALL ABOUT KING ARTHUR *by Geoffrey Ashe*   30p

552 54039 0   Carousel Non-Fiction

Arthur, King of Britain, became a national hero between the years of 1150-1200. The real ruler during most of that time was Henry II. But the legendary monarch was soon more widely renowned than the actual one . . . and his fame in romance has continued ever since.

How did the Arthurian legend begin, and in what forms have writers and poets presented it over the ages? Even more important are the questions: did King Arthur and his knights ever exist at all? How far are the stories true, how far are they invented? If any of the things happened, when did they happen?

Geoffrey Ashe explores both these paths. He traces the Arthur of fiction from the Middle Ages to the present day; he also tells the historical and archaeological facts of all that is known about the King.

DISCOVERERS AND ADVENTURERS *by R. J. Unstead*
30p

552 54031 5   Carousel Non-Fiction

R. J. Unstead has chosen some of the most exciting and intriguing discoverers and adventurers and tells their stories. Among the people he has written about are—John Cabot, who tried to find the North-West Passage, but failed; Lady Jane Grey who was Queen of England for only nine days; John Smith who was the real founder of Virginia; and William Dampier, the famous buccaneer.

EVERYDAY LIFE IN EARLY IMPERIAL CHINA
by Michael Loewe   35p

552 54043 9   Carousel Non-Fiction

What was it like to live in Imperial China during her first four centuries of greatness 2000 years ago? How did the emperor rule over 50 million inhabitants in over 100 administrative divisions?

Michael Loewe paints a full and vivid picture of the Han period (202 B.C.-A.D. 220). He describes the life of the peasants working the land, as well as the inhabitants of the towns—the rich, the tradesmen and artisans, the courtiers and officials, and the beggars and criminals. He examines their position in society, their work, their stints of government service—either as statutory labourers or in the army, their religious practices, and the elaborate hierarchy of institutions and civil servants who enforced the decisions of the imperial government.

LOUIS PASTEUR and The Fight Against Disease
by Richard Serjeant 25p

552 54042 0 Carousel Non-Fiction

This book tells the story of Louis Pasteur's many discoveries about disease and the further work that has been done since his death. It also tells the story of Pasteur's life and sets it against the life of his times. This makes clear the problems Pasteur faced, the way he was able to solve them, and the almost unbelievable changes that this brilliant man brought to the world of his day and ours.

THE HOW AND WHY WONDER BOOK OF DINOSAURS
25p

552 86501 X

Dinosaurs ruled the prehistoric earth for a period of 120 million years. The full story of these fierce, forbidding and fascinating monsters is retold in the best-selling book of the *How and Why* series. Packed with illustrations, many in full colour, this book tells all there is to know about dinosaurs.

THE HOW AND WHY WONDER BOOK OF THE TOWER OF LONDON
20p

552 86545 1

The Tower of London is one of Britain's most famous historical buildings. Today it is known for the crown jewels and the world-famous 'Beefeaters'. In the past it has housed Kings and Queens, and served as a prison for Sir Walter Raleigh, the 'Little Princes', and other well-known people. The full story of the Tower's past and present is retold in this book, with many illustrations.

THE HOW AND WHY WONDER BOOK OF EXTINCT ANIMALS 25p

552 86555 9

Here is a fabulous array of animals that have become extinct, from the early dinosaurs to more recent victims of man's actions. And there is also a warning: many species including pandas, tigers and leopards are in danger of disappearing, and the final question posed is ' Is the human race becoming extinct? '

THE ARABIAN NIGHTS: ALI BABA AND OTHER STORIES FROM THE THOUSAND AND ONE NIGHTS

THE ARABIAN NIGHTS: ALADDIN AND OTHER STORIES FROM THE THOUSAND AND ONE NIGHTS

by Amabel Williams-Ellis
2 Volumes 30p

552 52036 5
552 52037 3 Carousel Fiction

Long ago, there lived a powerful King. His beautiful Queen seemed to love him as dearly as he loved her; but one day he discovered that she had been conspiring with his enemies to poison him. Half-mad with rage, this King killed his treacherous Queen and vowed that each time he married, his new wife would be beheaded on the morning after the marriage. For some time the King kept his wicked vow. One day he ordered his Grand Vizier to bring him his eldest daughter, Shahrazad, to be his next Queen. Now Shahrazad was not only beautiful she also knew more than a thousand stories. She devised a plan using these stories to prolong her life and to stop the King fulfilling his vow. These two volumes include some of these tales.

HERACLES THE STRONG *by Ian Serraillier*   25p
552 52034 9   Carousel Fiction

Heracles was the son of Zeus, the Father of the gods, but he was born into a mortal family. The goddess Hera hated Heracles because he was not her own, and in a fit of spite and jealousy drove him blindly mad. Like a whirlwind Heracles raged through the palace and committed the most dreadful crimes.

Condemned by the gods, Heracles had no alternative but to accept his punishment and tackle the twelve seemingly impossible tasks set before him by the cowardly King Eurystheus.